Alexander De Croo

THE AGE OF WOMEN

**Why feminism
also liberates men**

ASP

Introduction

Pumped with adrenaline. That is how I felt in December 2018 when I stepped onto the Global Citizen Mandela 100 stage in Johannesburg. The FNB stadium – the largest in Africa – was filled with 90,000 enthusiastic South Africans, not only present for a concert, but also to support the Sustainable Development Goals. World-renowned performers like Beyoncé, Jay-Z, Pharrell Williams and Chris Martin took the stage … and I was handed the mic. My job: to get more attention for girls' and women's rights. I led 90,000 voices in chanting "She Is Equal" for a minute or two. My adrenaline surged. *She. Is. Equal!*

This was certainly an inflection point in my commitment to equal opportunities for girls and women. When I stepped off the stage, I realized that I had changed a lot in recent years. From an unconscious feminist to a vocal advocate of women's rights. For a long time, I lived in the belief that gender equality was not really an issue anymore. It was all perfectly arranged, especially in the West. In my family and in my environment, men and women are equal. Decisions are made together. Everyone is respected; nobody has the upper hand. Women are independent, have their own income and stand on their own two feet.

I have been surrounded by strong women my entire life. My mother studied law in the fifties, and later, she specialized in divorce law at her law firm. We cannot imagine this now, but divorces were quite rare in the rural area where I grew up. My mother noticed how women were frequently imprisoned by their marriage. Women were humiliated, beaten or cheated on and could not afford to leave their husbands. My mother always told them to look for a job and become financially independent. Only then would they be able to leave their husbands and take their destiny into their own hands. She got a lot of criticism for that attitude. A judge once tore into her to stop inciting young women to divorce; an attorney who stood up for a woman's right to make her own life choices was apparently inappropriate.

I met my wife at the international consulting firm where we both started our careers. It soon became clear to me that she was better suited for the job than I was. She quickly ascended – much faster than I did. Competing with my wife at the same company made no sense. I would not make it. It undoubtedly encouraged me to follow my childhood dream and start my own company.

First, however, I went to study in the United States for another two years. I was not married yet, but it was inconceivable for my now wife to accompany me as a non-working partner. She convinced her employer to transfer her to their Chicago office, where she continued her career path while I studied.

Once, my wife accepted an invitation from the university for the partners of students. She thought she would meet like-minded people and exchange professional experience. She ended up at a party where young women compared their wedding rings. *Never again*, she decided.

Being surrounded by strong women meant women's rights were a matter of fact. After all, the battle had been fought. *And won, right?* It seemed to me the great, historical achievements of feminism were obvious: women's suffrage, university admission, property rights, equal inheritance, the right to abortion, maternity leave, the criminalization of rape within marriages. I was by no means the only one who thought that feminism had reached its final destination.

There were still some problems, yes, I understood that. I had noticed that fewer women were able to climb to the top of business or politics, but at least we were on the right track. It would solve itself, I imagined; gender equality was within reach. For a long time, I was an oblivious feminist, a believer in total equality between men and women, but saw that it was no longer a point of contention. Militant feminism had achieved its goals and was no longer necessary. Simone de Beauvoir, she was someone from seventy years ago, right? And what was 'classic' feminism, anyway? Didn't the equality banner cover dozens of other issues by then, one more extreme than the other? Wasn't it understandable that the successful women in my circle of family and friends did not want anything to do with feminism? Too polarizing. The woman was too often the exploited victim; too intolerant, and too anti-man.

That was until four years ago, when – totally unexpectedly – I became the Belgian Minister for International Development. To immerse myself in the subject, I immediately went out into the field. In the countries I visited, I was haunted by the systematic oppression of women. I saw the face of hopelessness, and it was usually the face of a woman. I have discovered that, in large parts of the world, women are not independent at all.

An anecdote: a few months ago, I visited Senegal. We drove to a remote village two hours north of the capital Dakar. A large group of women was waiting for our delegation. When my car stopped, they started to sing, dressed up in the typical long colorful dresses that touch to the ground. They talked with animated gestures and radiated joy. They were proud, too. Instantly, they put me in a good mood. We were there to visit an agricultural project fully managed by these women. With the income they earn, they increase their independence and send their children to school.

We exited the car with our sleeves rolled up. It was hot, the sun blasted across my face. A man welcomed us, very formally, and explained in detail how good this project is for all these women. The women behind him were silent and stared at the ground. Only after I started making remarks and directly addressed the women, did he finally let a woman speak – much against his will. It is a scene I have experienced quite a few times in recent years. In a sewing workshop in South Sudan I saw the exact same pattern. Women run the local economy, put money in the bank, make sure the children go to school. And men have the last word and put the proverbial feathers in their caps.

It is women's stories that have hit me the hardest in recent years. In a refugee camp in Goma, in eastern Congo, I was met by a room full of women. Each had heartbreaking stories to tell about sexual violence perpetrated by Congolese soldiers and rebels. Or the woman in a refugee camp in Juba, South Sudan, who was threatened with rape every time she left the camp to gather wood or buy food.

In South Sudan we visited a remote village in the marshes, in the middle of the rebel area. We met young women, often girls, who hid in the swamp for weeks with their malnourished babies. An NGO gave them information about nutrition for young children. It had the most basic information: *how long should you breastfeed? What should you pay attention to?* In their society fragmented by civil war, these young mothers no longer had role models. Women and their babies are always the biggest victims of wars and conflicts.

These stories awakened me. I came to realize that women's rights are the key to development – and that there are still many barriers to acquiring these rights. Processes and networks everywhere prevent women from using their full potential. Ethically speaking it is unacceptable, and a huge waste. When men perpetuate their power and position at the expense of the other half of the population, the whole economy becomes impoverished and the entire society loses. "Empower women and the rest will follow," says investor and philanthropist Warren Buffett.

I evolved from an oblivious feminist into an aware one. It was a rude awakening. It took a trek across dozens of places on other continents to make me realize that gender inequality still exists. Not only in remote countries, but also with us in the Western world: the pay gap, the glass ceilings, the physical and sexual violence against women. The *manels*, panels that consist of only men, where I would have to explain policy in places like the United Nations, the World Bank, the OECD, the European Union. Everywhere I went, I ended up in debates in which men explain, and afterwards women are allowed to ask questions. Men talk about women, but women are not given the chance. It will not happen to me anymore. I will no longer participate in *manels*.

This book is a report of my process (lasting several years) of becoming aware. It happened through events that shook me out of my slumber. #MeToo was quite a shock for many of us. Even environments with a strongly developed sense of ethos are not immune to sexual misconduct. The artistic world and the humanitarian aid sector's flagrancies, to name but two. Or the discovery that Flemish universities are bastions of gender inequality. Or the discovery that a company with a substantial government interest (and one that I am in charge of) does not have a single woman on its management team.

Gradually, I also started to realize that we are just not moving forward. Elif Shafak, the successful author of Turkish descent, is right when she states that history is sometimes also put into reverse. There is a man in the White House who claims that he can grope women in their crotch and move on them "like a bitch" to have sex with impunity. In the authoritarian regimes on the edge of Europe, populism and women-unfriendly policies go hand in hand. Just look at Turkey or Russia. Just as it is in the United States, the right to abortion is also under pressure in various conservative countries in Europe, like Poland. In the United Kingdom, two women are murdered by their partners every week. In Belgium, eight reports of rape are made every day, which almost never lead to a conviction. The number of women in top positions, both in politics and in the business world, has stopped increasing and hovers at about a third. Women still lose out to men, in companies, at universities, in sport, culture, politics.

This will come back and bite us. This century is the most

disruptive ever. Artificial intelligence. Global warming. Globalization and migration. The ageing population in industrialized countries. The population explosion in emerging countries. We might not make it. Perhaps global warming is completely out of hand. Maybe we will not get mass migration under control. Perhaps the fourth industrial revolution will lead to massive job losses and social security will become unaffordable. It all can happen, some believe.

Personally, I disagree. I am convinced that we will make it, thanks to our creativity and technology, but on one condition. Our society, our prosperity, and our economy can only survive the coming storms if the role of women in our society and economy expands – significantly. If we mobilize the entire world population, we can make it. To date, the talent and potential of the female half of the population remain under-utilized.

Long-term and sustainable economic growth is only possible if we make optimal use of all talent, both male and female. Women contribute only 37% to the gross global product, the sum of all goods and services produced throughout the world. If women were to contribute as much to the economy as men, this would add $28 trillion to the gross global product. A dizzying amount, the same as the combined economies of the United States and China.

Within the OECD, the Organization for Economic

Co-operation and Development, the employment rate is 75% for men and 60% for women. The OECD is the club of most industrialized countries minus China and India. If three-quarters of the women had a job, as is the case with men, this would result in an additional economic growth of 12%. Women with jobs have an income. In turn, they consume and create employment – and prosperity. It is not a zero-sum game where an extra job for a woman automatically means one less for a man.

We can no longer afford the waste of talent and prosperity. The challenge for the following decades is to drastically change the infrastructure of our economies and societies, so that women have the opportunity to enter the formal labor market and contribute equally to wealth creation.

In this book, I argue to give women a real choice: a real choice about the subject they want to study; the profession they want to pursue; the man or woman they desire as a partner; the number of children they want (or the choice not to have children at all); the way they want to combine their careers with their personal lives; the extent to which they want to take on the care tasks within their family (or not).

Women do not have that true freedom of choice, or not enough, not even in my own country. Traditions, habits, social pressure, upbringing, role models – they all limit women's options, pushing them in a particular direction. Women only really have the freedom to choose when men are willing to make the same choices. *As long as true freedom of choice does not exist, women cannot be equal to men.*

In the following chapters, I will lay out how to tackle this problem on the basis of a number of questions. How do we change the stereotypes that restrict women and men to narrow social roles? Why do women end up in subordinate positions or in undervalued occupations where they earn less? How do we make the labor market flexible so that fewer women get stuck in either part-time jobs or unpaid, housebound work? How can more men opt for a better balance between career and family? Why is it better for women to have children at the beginning of their careers? Why should we lower the school age? Why is it more important for companies to have more women in their executive teams than on their boards? Are quotas a necessary evil? How can women play their full role in the economy, increase their society's prosperity and enforce social change? How can we adjust the economic balance between women and men and use this as a catalyst for gender equality? Why is the gender pay gap such a good indicator of a country's gender equality? Why should we focus on the "zero wage gap" in the coming years in order to realize equality between women and men?

The answers to these questions are quite confronting, even for me. I am certainly not the perfect example of what we have to do. In our family, it is my wife who works part-time to help manage the kids, not me. More men than women work in my cabinet and my three heads of cabinet are male. The secretarial duties are administered by a woman, my ministerial chauffeur is a man. There is a palpable difference between my words and my actions, I am well aware. But I'm trying to make that difference smaller. It will be work for the long-term. The following chapters form a how-to manual, also for me.

By the way, who am I to bring up the topic at all? Am I not the umpteenth man who thinks he knows everything, like that man in that village in Senegal, like all the men in those *manels*? It's called *mansplaining*, this need men have to explain anything and everything to women, even the things women know much more about. The American author Rebecca Solnit wrote about how a man wanted to explain the moral essence of a book—a book that she had written herself. He needed to be told three or four times that she was the author before he would stop, too.

And yet, I feel that I must tell this story in my role as a government leader and an allied male voice. I am an imperfect advocate, but must we wait for a perfect one to begin the new phase in the fight for gender equality? Now that legal equality is almost a fact, at least in the Western hemisphere, it is time to make social and economic equality a reality: as many women in top positions as men; as many women in computer science and technology as men; as many men in health care, in part-time work and in the household as women. Men doing these things without being bothered or ridiculed. For men must also be liberated from the traditions, habits, social pressure, upbringing and role models that force them in a certain direction. Men must also be able to choose, for example, for a better balance between career and personal life.

It will be quite a challenge to turn this century into the Age of Women, the century in which inequality between men and women is wiped out once and for all. Declaring an International Women's Year, as the United Nations did in 1975, will not suffice to get us there. Nor will the yearly International Women's Day on March 8. No, it will require a much more sustained effort, for many decades to come. Whether we manage to reach true gender equality will depend on women increasing their contribution to economic prosperity and social well-being, on men allowing women a free choice and on men making free choices themselves. That is the challenge for all men calling themselves feminists. And I am one of them.

Brussels, March 2019

The Gender Pay Gap

Women earn less than men. Among the OECD countries, the average is 14% less. Romania has a difference of a mere 1.5% between women and men. My home country, Belgium, landed a respectable fourth place: a Belgian woman earns on average 4.7% less than a Belgian man. The United States and the United Kingdom score worse than average with gender pay gaps of 16.8% and 18.2% respectively. South Korea is a straggler; women earn *a third* less than men. The World Bank calculated that the difference in wages costs \$160 trillion every year. Moreover, losses for women are highest in Europe and the US because wages are so high.

The concept of the gender pay gap continues to bear a stubborn misconception. A 4% pay gap does not mean that women are paid 4% less than men for the same work, rather that men are paid 4% more than women in general. The wage gap is calculated by dividing the average wages of men by the average wages of women.

Where does this difference come from? Sheryl Sandberg, Facebook's second-in-command, believes that women negotiate their salary less vigorously than men. When she joined Facebook, she was inclined to immediately accept Mark Zuckerberg's first proposal. Sandberg's husband convinced her to counter with a higher number. When she did so, Zuckerberg put a significantly more generous offer on the table.

The gender pay gap is a result of more than just the differences in negotiation techniques between men and women. It is also a perfect indicator of the inequalities between men and women, because it lies at the juncture of so many crucial dimensions: gender norms, prejudice and discrimination, the proportion of women in unpaid and part-time work, different education and career choices, and the number of women in top jobs.

23

Not all gender pay gaps are the result of discrimination. A male Uber driver earns seven percent more. Due to the algorithms employed, driver selection is gender neutral, since selecting "male" or "female" is not an option when ordering an Uber. Half of the 7% pay gap is due to the fact that Uber men drive faster and complete more rides in an hour. Men also drive more frequently at night when the rates are higher. They are more likely to drive through dangerous neighborhoods, which also results in higher rates. And they perform more hours, build up more experience, and so know the best routes for the most lucrative rides. The wage gap at Uber is not due to discrimination, but due to greater risk-taking, availability and flexibility.

If the gender pay gap is a means to measuring inequality, then the "zero wage gap" is the goal. A zero wage gap indicates that there is no longer any difference in the average wages between men and women. This implies that an equal number of men and women opt for part-time or unpaid work, an equal number of women and men are in better paying jobs, and women contribute the same degree to economic growth and wellbeing as men. The zero wage gap is a positive indicator, which is why it is used as the objective throughout this entire book.

Women earning less than men for the same work is the result of genuine discrimination in only a limited number

The Gender Pay Gap

of cases. Yet, this gender pay gap is very stubborn, as a result of three factors:

First, too many women work part-time. In the European Union, nearly one in three women work part-time, while only 8% of men do. In Belgium, it is 44% of women compared to 11% percent of men. In Germany, the ratio is even more imbalanced. Almost seven out of ten women with children work part-time, while only 6% of fathers do so. This not only leads to a significant gender pay gap, but also to higher poverty rates in older women – and this in a country that has been led by a female Chancellor for almost fifteen years, no less.

A gender-neutral society is exactly that: one with no difference between men and women in the labour market. Some argue that the high number of women in part-time work is the result of choice. I do not agree; women do not voluntarily opt for part-time work – at least not to the current extent. Rather, women often feel they are forced into that choice. Conversely, men who want to work part-time encounter obstacles and prejudices that likewise make it difficult to do so.

In Belgium, for example, we give a particularly strange signal as a government. With measures called *a marriage quotient*, we give tax support to single-income families: 30% of the income of the partner who works outside the home is considered income of the stay-at-home partner. It can yield a tax bonus of up to €5,000 per year. But it can also be a reason for the stay-at-home partner not venturing into formal employment. How striking that our tax system does not offer tax support for families where both partners balance work and private life. On top of this, our tax system is particularly disadvantageous for single parents, a vulnerable group consisting mainly of mothers. Other countries also have similar mechanisms with the same result: women are discouraged from having their own job.

Secondly, too few women work in sectors that pay well, such as computer science and technology. Occupations that directly benefit society are economically undervalued – which happen to be jobs and sectors that many women choose, such as those in the education or care professions.

Thirdly, too few women reach leadership positions due to the assumption that household responsibilities and childcare mean they will not be available to the extent required by the position. It is worth noting that when we imagine these top functions, we simply do not take women into account the same way we do men. Take politics as an example, a field in which overly macho culture still dominates. An agreement cannot be a good one unless it is reached after long meetings late into the night. We have to design politics differently. It would benefit not only women, but also men. They have to invest in their families too.

I think if there were as many women as men in government, things would be different. The rules would change, especially if those women still had school-aged children. They would not accept evening meetings. They would probably also end our ritual of holding meetings: first feeling out the different viewpoints, followed by some sort of theatrical discussion, and then ending in a nighttime agreement and press interviews at dawn.

As Deputy Prime Minister and member of the government, I myself have participated in these rituals in recent years. My wife's eyes grow big in amazement. Is an agreement reached at four in the morning better than one made at five in the afternoon? All top-level politicians pay a price for this. We are not enough present within our families. I am too often an absent father, even though I do my best to take my sons to school twice a week and watch their football matches during the weekend.

Venus or Mars?

In his controversial 1992 book *Men Are from Mars, Women Are from Venus*, the American relationship therapist John Gray posits that women and men behave quite differently; they hold different ambitions and objectives. They express their emotions, their desires, in a different way. They even speak a different language – as if they come from two different planets.

The planets that Gray selected are not coincidental; he chose Mars, the Roman *god* of war and Venus, the *goddess* of love. The book was a phenomenal success, one of the best-selling non-fiction books of all time. But it also received a lot of criticism because it reduced women and men to characteristics that are innate, genetically determined, and where there is not much that can be changed.

I do not believe in the Venus and Mars myth. Women and men differ, indeed, both biologically and psychologically. But those differences are smaller than generally assumed. And often such differences are due to upbringing, social pressure, tradition and religion rather than being innate. Besides, both men and women often differ between one another more than with each other. Who would differ the most? The male and female from Naples? Or the male from Naples and the male from Helsinki? I think the men from Naples and Helsinki differ more, even though they are both men. And we intuitively understand why: the different societies and cultures in which they were born, live, work, and love.

NBC, the American television and radio network, conducted a large-scale opinion poll asking about the main reason for the differences between men and women. More than half felt that social factors and societal causes were the basis. A third thought it was biology. The rest opted for a combination of both. Of course, women and men have organic differences from each other. They play a different role in reproduction. Men are larger and have more muscle strength. There are also brain differences. Men's brains are on average 10% to 12% larger than those of women. Does this mean something? Only that larger brain size is related to controlling a larger body – not intelligence or cognitive ability.

There are countless studies about the brains of men and women; Google gives three million hits on the topic. But does that say anything about intelligence? There *are* differences in brain wiring. More connections occur within each hemisphere in men. In women, both hemispheres work better together, and the bundle of nerves that connects both brain halves is thicker. It explains why women can multitask better. More and more studies point in that direction. Women are better than men when performing simultaneous tasks or tasks in rapid succession. In doing so, women tend to work with a more thought-out approach, based on a well-defined strategy, while men tend to work more impulsively.

According to some, the difference in approach is the result of hundreds of thousands of years' worth of evolution. For millennia, men were warriors and hunters. That would explain why they excel in spatial skills. Women took care of the household. They patched their husband's clothes while keeping an eye out to make sure their toddler's hands did not touch the fire, where the stew was simmering. In short, they multi-tasked.

I enjoy reading these studies. It gives me great pleasure clicking from link to link, jumping from one article to the next. I like it all. Yet sometimes it makes me laugh. The great spatial insight that men have thanks to our warrior and hunter history would explain why we can now use maps or park better. The fact that women had to feed, wash and dress husband and offspring all the time explains why they communicate better. Surely, it's true to a certain extent. But how relevant is that information? How are we, in the year 2019, better off with all of that map reading and car parking, now that smart cars can take over these tasks?

Now, no matter what, greater muscle strength and brain size does not protect men against the most important gender gap of all: the life expectancy gap.

In a recent report, Duke University published a mortality study of seven humanitarian crises over the past 250 years. Famines in Ukraine, Sweden and Ireland. Slavery in Trinidad. The return of freed slaves to Liberia. Two epidemics of measles in Iceland. In each of those seven catastrophes, the women survived better than the men. This was true even for newborns. During the famine of the 1930s in Ukraine, newborn girls had a life expectancy of 11 years, compared to 7.5 for boys. Even in the most life-threatening circumstances, the study concluded that women's chances of survival are greater than men's.

Since 1980, women have lived longer than men on all continents. They are biologically better equipped for longevity in part due to the presence of two X chromosomes instead of an X and a Y chromosome. With two X chromosomes, women have a duplicate from each gene. This is useful when something goes wrong with one of these genes as a result of mutation. Men do not have that backup.

The dominant sex hormones also play an important role. Estrogen protects women against certain conditions, such as high cholesterol, while testosterone lowers life expectancy in men. After numerous experiments had shown that male animals live longer after castration, biologists wondered whether this was also the case with humans. For years this remained a theoretical discussion, because it was too controversial to determine with actual experiments. That was until the Korean scientist Han-Nam Park, together with his colleagues, examined the nineteenth century medical data of 81 eunuchs at the Imperial Court in Korea. Their testicles, the center of testosterone production, were removed before puberty. They lived on average twenty years longer than the other men in the palace, including the Emperors. The conclusion drawn from this was that men live shorter lives because of their testosterone.

But biology and behavior complement each other. Behavioral factors are at least as important as biological ones in explaining women's greater life expectancy. Men eat less healthily. They smoke more, drink more, and take more drugs. They also fight more often. It is usually men who go to battle in war, uprisings and terrorist networks. It comes at a high price: more lung cancer and liver cirrhosis, more deadly stab wounds and shooting incidents, more soldiers killed.

We all know men, especially young ones, who cause accidents because of their reckless behavior. Three-quarters of road fatalities are of men; excessive speed and driving under the influence of alcohol or drugs are the two main causes. A study by the Belgian Institute for Traffic Safety shows that women being drunk behind the wheel or driving too fast happens less often.

Or take Russian men – they live 13 years less than Russian women. In 1999, an international group of researchers interviewed 151,000 Russian men about their lifestyle. Ten years later, they looked these men up again. Eight thousand had died. There was only one explanation according to the researchers: vodka. Much too much vodka. Three or more bottles per week.

The differences in brain structure and functioning are too small to make pronounced conclusions about the behavior of men and women. Behavior has as much to do with social phenomena as with biological factors. And that's how we end up with gender standards. Women and men are forced into gender roles from birth, under the influence of upbringing, education, social pressure and social expectations.

Pink or Blue?

Gender norms are the standards of behavior considered normal and appropriate for men and women. Doctors are men, and nurses women. Directors are men and secretaries are women. This last gender role is also fully established in linguistic terms: everyone understands the concept behind 'secretary'. That is, until you speak about *a* 'Secretary'. I wonder what will happen to that word once Antonio Guterres, the Secretary-General of the United Nations, is succeeded by a woman (it is about time, by the way).

Fortunately, these standards are evolving. Doctors are no longer all men. The profession is becoming less gendered, at an increasingly rapid pace. Male nurses, however, still remain a small minority in most hospitals and nursing homes.

What we do not realize, or want to realize, is that gender norms start from birth, or even before, when gender is determined. If it is a girl, then the first pink baby clothes are purchased, while for a boy, it's blue onesies. Later, girls get dolls, which they can change or bottle feed themselves. Then comes the play kitchen, the tea set. From their first years of life it is made clear what is expected of them: taking care of the household and children. We play 'house' and hold 'tea parties' so they know who will have to fix the meals. Rather quickly, girls will also get make-up sets and plastic jewelry. Their appearance is important, of course. Mothers will teach them to iron, to sew a knot, and separate the woolen clothes from the cottons.

Boys get cars, trains, tractors, trucks, dinosaurs, building blocks and mechanical kits. Revolvers, rifles and cowboy suits, too. Later they are told that the household repair tasks are 'a man's job'. Fathers teach them how to mow the lawn, replace a broken lamp, hammer a nail into the wall.

Perhaps you now think: *What does it matter whether they play with a doll or with a truck?* It says nothing about their later lives. True. But gender norms are the starting point for inequality and discrimination. They have an influence over the studies that girls and boys pursue, the professions they choose, the extent to which they push through to the top in business or politics.

Gender norms are by definition unconscious. Based on prejudices and assumptions, they have their roots in culture, tradition, customs, faith and superstition. Actually, we would prefer not be confronted with them. They are such a common occurrence that we gladly accept that others do it, just not us. *Muslims, they are the ones who treat their wives badly.* That sort of reasoning.

Stereotyping based on gender is deeply rooted and age-old, though not always visible. It has far-reaching consequences, such as in selection and recruitment. More men than women play in symphony orchestras. Is this because fewer women study music than men? No. Is it because women play music less well than men? Also no. Why then? Because people unconsciously assume that men are better musicians. In a blind selection, when the musician is not visible and the name is not known, just as many women as men are selected.

In an experiment with university professors, 63 men and 64 women had to assess several candidates for a laboratory director position. All candidates had the required skills;

the only variable was gender. The male candidates' qual-
ifications were estimated significantly higher, and their
suggested starting salary was on average $4,000 high-
er. Even more striking: there was no appreciable difference between the assessments performed by the female
professors and their male colleagues. The women also
showed a substantial prejudice to the detriment of their
own gender.

I read another study about recruitment based on identical
CVs. Handsome men are approached twice as often by
a selection agency than less attractive ones. But pretty
women are approached up to six times more often than
those deemed less so. Women are judged more often by
their appearance than men in a selection process. On
Google, the search query *"Is my son a genius?"* is entered
twice as often as the same about a daughter. These are
all examples of unconscious bias, not conscious decisions.

Just how deeply ingrained these gender norms are in all of
us can be seen in an experiment by the British broadcaster BBC (available to watch on YouTube): infant boys
are dressed like girls, and infant girls like boys. A bat-
tery of professional supervisors are then sent to them.
With the so-called girls, they head towards the dolls.
With the 'boys', the cars. Not the children – the *adults*.
When confronted with their own actions after the test,

the supervisors were horrified. They never thought that even they would fall into the trap of gender stereotypes.

Last year the United Nations' Entity for Gender Equality and the Empowerment of Women, UN Women, and 24 global corporations including Mars, Microsoft and Johnson & Johnson, formed an alliance to end stereotypical gender roles. The initiative was started by Unilever, the second largest advertiser in the world, which has already trained eighty thousand employees on this topic.

The feminine hygiene brand, Always, took it to heart. In the award-winning advertising campaign *Like a Girl*, women exposing their perfect teeth are replaced by hesitant adolescents searching for self-confidence. Failure is part of growing up, it seems to say, the message being, "So let's keep failing. Because we only truly fail when we don't even try."

American linguists have analyzed the dialogue of twelve classic Walt Disney cartoons. Of compliments given to girls and women, about 60% are for their beauty, and only 10% their skills. In *Snow White*, the main character's beauty is the whole point of the story. It is the first Disney film in a series with the 'damsel in distress' theme: a becoming lady is in trouble until a handsome prince saves her.

In recent Disney films, the helpless female premise has changed, and now the story is as much about their talents as their appearance. The two female protagonists in *Frozen* are strong, independent women who do not need a handsome prince to give meaning to their lives.

You are born a boy or girl (usually, anyway). But you become a man or woman by the way others treat you, by the toys, books, clothes and role models they throw at you, and by thousands of other tiny acts that propel you in a certain direction; steered towards a certain study, profession, and income. *Unconsciously.*

The American sociologist Elizabeth Sweet researched the 7,300 toys that had been included in the Sears catalog over the past century. For decades, toys unmistakably confirmed gender norms. Feeling pressure from the feminist movement, it changed in the 1970s. Only 2% of the toys were gender-specific. But the pendulum swung back the other way a few years later. It was very unfortunate, according to Sweet. For adults, toys are for leisure. But for children, they are a vital learning tool that prepares for later life. What is learned while young remains well into our later years.

What has to change? First among many: the books we put in the hands of young children, including textbooks. More books in which the father does the dishes and the mother washes the car. The household duties and caretaking tasks within a family should no longer be divided solely according to gender. Parents must teach daughters to do repairs and sons how to iron.

In Swedish education, household lessons such as cooking and sewing belong to the standard curriculum of all children, including boys. We have to invest more in guiding study and career choices, with counselors who are well aware of the impact of gender norming. Teachers must receive training in recognizing gender norms. And we must dare to speak up about the position in which girls and women find themselves in families with immigrant roots. What these girls see at home is sometimes at odds with what they learn at school. Girls are married off too young, or have their genitals mutilated in our Western countries, also.

While preparing for this book, I spoke with a good friend of mine, an executive, about the relationship between men and women in his company. During the conversation he came to the realization that he always gave his most important or difficult assignments to a male employee. He had never thought about it before. He never did it consciously, but suddenly he fixed it. He was shocked. Gender equality is important to him. Not a single woman in his company had ever spoken to him about it. Society brainwashes women from birth so that they find it normal to play second fiddle.

Another example. From time to time, my wife's employer, a large international consulting firm, organizes meetings to which the partners of staff members are also invited. Sometimes I go along. When we are approached as a couple, they ask me which department I lead; my wife is automatically assumed to be the significant other, since she is a woman.

Prejudices are unconscious, but they are sustained by habits and customs. In this way, religions continue a tradition of gender inequality. When religions discriminate against women, it is not surprising that societies do the same. You see this in sport, for example. Prize money in the most important tennis tournaments or marathon competitions is now the same for men and women. But in football (soccer) or cycling, women earn only a fraction of their male counterparts. This is starting to change, too, however.

In Norway, the men and women of the national soccer team earn the same amount. But in many other countries, a similar demand from the female soccer elite falls on deaf ears. It could change, now that interest in the women's game is on the rise.

Gender norming is particularly tough and painful for men and women whose bodies do not conform to the standard, such as those who identify as transgender. The feeling that you are trapped in the wrong body, while also experiencing the pressure to behave according to your birth gender – how heavy must that be? I am reminded of Bo Van Spilbeeck. Bo, aged 59, had been a highly re-garded foreign affairs journalist for a Belgian television broadcaster over the past twenty years, albeit as a man and under the name of Boudewijn.

After a lifetime of suppressing her transgender identity and fighting against dark thoughts, Bo decided to come out as transgender and make her transformation public. There was little negative reaction. Only a few right-wing ex-tremists argued that changing gender does not say any-thing about guts and character, but rather is a surrender to eccentric fantasies. Luckily, they were a tiny minority.

Incidentally, and true to stereotype, during a TV interview, Bo assured us that she would try to do better as a jour-nalist than before. Because, she added, "a woman must always prove herself twice, right?"

"She has figured that out already," the interviewer re-marked tersely.

A Deadly Pandemic

In Africa, I always notice that you see so few girls on the street. "Where are the girls?" I ask myself every time I visit countries such as Senegal, Benin or Uganda. It turns out that girls stay home to help their mothers or go to the fields, while the boys play outside.

When I go to the Middle East or North Africa, I do not see women in the tea houses. Again, these are expressions of gender norms influenced by culture, tradition and religion. In these societies, women do not belong in public places. They have to take care of the household, the children and the elderly. They are also forbidden from causing men to have lewd thoughts and are condemned to a life in the shadows.

We can see what prejudices lead to in China, India and Southeast Asia. In these countries, 1.5 million girls are never born, or are killed at birth. Every year. Girls are denied life just because they are girls. One would expect this number to drop, but the opposite is true. The number of abortions of female fetuses increases as ultrasound technology improves, so much so that the Indian government forbids the fetal gender to be revealed during an ultrasound.

Tradition and culture play an important role in this phenomenon. A son is counted on to continue the family line. Daughters are considered a burden, a bad investment, because of the dowry that must be paid later. It is assumed that boys will earn more than girls, and so can take better care of their parents when they are elderly.

In northern Vietnam, only the sons are allowed to go in their parents' funerals; it is a condition for wellbeing in the afterlife. In China, the one-child policy has averted a devastating population explosion, but at the expense of tens of millions of girls' lives. The consequences for the whole society are disruptive: the lack of women who are able to marry has in turn lead to kidnappings and rape. Incidentally, it is difficult to eradicate the practice. Chinese and Indian migrants in the United States regularly opt for an abortion when a fetus is found to be a girl. Some cultures allow for their daughters to be killed. Quite a few cultures allow mutilation. According to UNICEF, 200 million women in the world have experienced genital mutilation. In countries such as Somalia or Guinea, nearly all women are maimed in this way. Female circumcision also occurs in Europe, where some migrants continue the practice. The United Kingdom and Germany are just a few of the surprising countries that populate this list. In Belgium, there are 18,000 circumcised women, with 8,000 girls at risk of being circumcised – often occurring when they return to the country of their family's origin for a visit. But increasingly, immigrant groups bring someone, almost always a women, to their new countries to circumcise the girls. In many cultures, girls are murdered or maimed. But they are mistreated in *all* cultures. "Hit your wife every day. You may not know why, but she will," is a saying reputed by some to be of Arabic origin, while others say it is Chinese. Whatever the origin, few proverbs are so meticulously put into practice as this one. According to the World Health Organization, one in three women are victims of physical or sexual violence in the course of their lives. One in eight is sexually assaulted, one in twenty raped.

One billion women, that is what we are speaking about. According to the World Bank, one of the worst pandemics in history, gender violence, is a plague all over the globe. The murders, the rapes, the beatings, the bullying, the threats, the intimidations. The cost is dizzyingly high: devastated lives, disability, depression and long-term illnesses, aborted careers, long periods of absence from work. In addition to the immense human suffering, there are also the economic costs, which the World Bank estimates to be 4% of the gross global product.

If men stopped killing, raping, hitting, bullying, threatening and intimidating women, the economy would grow by 4%. Four percent for the European economy would mean €670 billion (US $788 billion), or roughly the entire GDP of Switzerland. That could pay for a lot of the gender-friendly proposals that I formulate in this book: longer paternity leave, cheaper childcare or starting primary school at a younger age, for example.

In two-thirds of cases, the violent perpetrator is the partner or an ex-partner. Women are most often attacked at home. The most dangerous place for a woman is not a poorly-lit parking garage or a lonely bicycle path along a canal, but her own home. Every year, 40,000 domestic violence complaints come to the police in our country,

Belgium. That's 110 per day. Two out of three complaints are dismissed, which means that the public prosecutor has decided not to charge anyone. Of the 40,000 complaints, only 40 cases lead to a temporary order to leave the home and a restraining order for the perpetrator. In only 4% of the reported rapes does filing a report lead to a conviction. Belgium was called out by the United Nations for this scandalously low figure.

We are not only dealing with a pandemic, we are also hardly doing anything about it. Action starts with no longer accepting stereotypes that perpetuate women as stupid or reduces them to disposable lust objects.

Stopping the pandemic of violence against women and taking a stand against female-unfriendly stereotypes also means telling positive stories about women. That happens far too little. It is men who record history; the role women play is overlooked. Eighty percent of the biographies on Wikipedia are about men. Eighty percent of the obituaries that *The New York Times* publishes memorialize men.

You see the same trend in street names. In Montreal, only six percent of the 6,000 place names refer to women, while about half refer to men. Two years ago, in honor of its 375th anniversary, the city of Montreal rightly launched an effort to create a database of 375 prominent women to close this gap. In 2015, a feminist group protested the gender gap in the Paris street names; only 2.6% of the street names in the French capital refer to women. And then a large segment of them refer to the wives or daughters of famous men. Other world cities do not fare much better. In Rome, barely 3.5% of street names are linked to a woman. "Because the men made history," a news commentator said. *Really?*

#MeToo

In 1991, U.S. President George H. W. Bush nominated a black judge, Clarence Thomas, to the Supreme Court. The president appoints the judge, and the Senate confirms their nomination. During the hearings, a former staffer to the judge, Anita Hill, accused him of sexual misconduct. As so often is the case when a woman takes on a powerful man, she was heavily attacked and her credibility was questioned. It was Hill that faced a grilling, not Judge Thomas. The Senate approved his appointment.

In 2018, history repeated itself with the appointment of Brett Kavanaugh. While Christine Blasey Ford, Kavanaugh's victim, received much support from a broad cross-section of American society, President Trump brutally ridiculed her during a campaign event. On Twitter (where else?), he mocked her as not being credible. A nice piece of *victim blaming*, slandering the victim, as was also seen with one of Trump's predecessors.

"That woman," Bill Clinton said contemptuously at the news conference denying his sexual affair with intern Monica Lewinsky. I never understood why the entire political, cultural and intellectual elite, including women, stood behind Bill Clinton. They had no good word for the mistreated intern because their opponents were Republicans, who must not win. *Too bad for the intern.* But weren't higher interests at play? *And she should have said no, right?* They were consenting adults? *Didn't she bring this on herself?* All that mess with those semen stains on that blue dress. Shouldn't she have paid attention?

In one episode of the hilarious sketch *What Were You Wearing* on the BBC, a man has been robbed. He had a knife held to his throat and had to give up his watch and his smartphone. He files a report at the police station. The inspector comes in. A woman, the comedian Tracey Ullman.

"What did you wear during that robbery?" she begins.

"You're dressed flashy, don't you think? Expensive suit, nice shoes, flashy smartphone. In that neighborhood? You did provoke it yourself, did you not? You do understand that you are partly responsible for what happened to you. Did you have a drink, by the way?"

The man sits bewildered in his chair and stammers that he had a knife held to his throat. I think it is a beautiful sketch, perfectly summarizing the questions women are subjected to when they report a rape.

Societies evolve, but not evenly or linearly. It happens with fits and starts, with accelerations and sputters. I did not know that a journalist from *The New York Times*, Sharon Waxman, had already investigated in 2004 the many rumors about sexual misconduct by Harvey Weinstein, one of the most powerful men in Hollywood. Weinstein got a whiff of it and convinced the editor-in-chief not to publish it.

Thirteen years later, the newspaper would write about the same film producer who abused his position of power to forcibly molest or rape women. The news hit like a bomb, even though in the following weeks it was revealed that a lot of people had been aware for a long time. But Weinstein held a position in Hollywood that allowed him to make or break careers. Actresses feared that they would not get roles if they did not respond to his proposals.

While Tarana Burke started using the hashtag #MeToo a decade earlier, the actress Alyssa Milano launched it across Twitter. She called on all victims of sexual violence not to remain silent. A few days later, half a million women posted a tweet with that hashtag. World-famous actresses – Gwyneth Paltrow, Uma Thurman, Jennifer Lawrence, Salma Hayek, Reese Witherspoon, among others – testified about the sexual misconduct with which they had been confronted.

The scandals were not limited to the film world. Sports, theater, politics and television all appeared to be places where sexual intimidation thrives. Everywhere, giants tumbled from their pedestals.

To my dismay, as Minister of Development Cooperation, I was confronted with it myself when the world of humanitarian aid was not spared, either. I found it utterly disgusting how aid workers could abuse their position of power and commit sexual misconduct – at Oxfam, at Doctors Without Borders (MSF), during various United Nations peacekeeping operations.

As a Minister, you order an audit, you tighten the integrity procedures and you create transparency. But it still makes you feel nauseated and powerless at the thought of so much breached trust.

The avalanche of testimonies did not come easily. Something

had been going on for years. Revelations about child abuse in the Catholic Church had paved the way. *The Boston Globe* exposed the systemic molestations within the diocese in that city, as well as the systematic concealment and protection. The newspaper argued that the Church attracts predatory men who know that they will be able to go about their business with impunity.

Several incidents acted as harbingers of what was coming. Dominique Strauss-Kahn of the International Monetary Fund was accused of assaulting a hotel housekeeper. He fled, only to be escorted off the plane and arrested. Brock Turner, an up-and-coming swimmer at Stanford University, brutally assaulted with intent to rape an unconscious woman and received a particularly light prison sentence of six months. In a petition, more than a million Americans asked to remove the presiding judge from the bench. He was voted out in June 2018.

Jacqueline Sauvage, who killed her husband after 47 years of abuse, received a pardon from President Hollande. Jyoti Singh Pandey, an Indian woman, was raped by six men on a bus in New Delhi, and subsequently died from her injuries. Her torture showed how much Indian society is steeped in violence against women. Millions of women protested against Trump's sexual misconduct the day after his inauguration – it was the biggest single-day protest in American history. Larger than the marches against the Vietnam War. Larger than the marches against racial discrimination.

Suddenly there was a tidal wave of #MeToo testimonies showing that women have had enough. (Many men, too, by the way). In such a heated climate, exaggerated reactions are inevitable. After a few cases of sexual harassment and abuse of power, the rector of a Belgian university called upon professors to no longer conduct one-on-one meetings behind closed doors. The doors must remain open until the construction of exam and meeting rooms with a glass wall. The rector received blow back for this.

To warn others about an impending new prudishness, hundreds of women led by Cathérine Deneuve told *Le Monde* rape is always a crime, but flirting and seduction, however awkward at times, is not. Women and men must not allow #MeToo to hold us hostage to a new puritanism that catapults us back to Victorian times and confines women. Anne Morelli, a Belgian historian who signed the open letter, went a step further. There are women who are willing to do anything for a film role. It is not a black-and-white story of dirty pigs à la Weinstein and the innocent, defenseless creatures. Resilience, that is what it is all about, she said. Women need to be more assertive.

There are always discussions about boundaries when something that has been tolerated for centuries is suddenly no longer accepted. Men and women are seeking a new standard for ways to deal with each other, in terms of what is and what is not permissible. Can a politician, who will become a minister years later, put his hand on the knee of a female journalist? A former British Minister of Defense now knows that you had better not do that. Was there abuse of power? An inappropriate advance in exchange for an interview or a scoop? Or an inappropriate advance, period?

One thing has to be clear: whistleblowers deserve protection and anonymity if they seek it. At the same time, we have to make sure that #MeToo does not evolve into a witch hunt, with social media acting as a public trial. To avoid #MeToo leading to excess, we have to go back to the essence – abuse of power.

In all environments in which I have worked, I have witnessed relationships between colleagues. Sometimes between bosses and co-workers. Short affairs and long romances. *Do we want to ban this completely?* As long as there is no issue of abuse of power, there is no problem.

The line is crossed when a person in a dominant position adds sex into the equation and a job is put on the line. Or a promotion. Or human necessities. The film producer who connects a role to a blow-job. The manager who confuses sexual intimidation with employee evaluation. The humanitarian aid worker who buys sexual favors with a bowl of rice.

What we are experiencing is not a sudden epidemic of line-crossing behavior. Unfortunately, that has been there all along. It is the tolerance threshold that has been drastically reduced, combined with women's greater determination to no longer suffer this abuse of power.

#MeToo is a new benchmark. When the tectonic plates of what is and will not be accepted begin to shift, things can change fast. The scantily-clad women disappear at the car showroom; the same for the pit girls at Formula One, and the podium hostesses at cycling races and ladies in bikinis between boxing match rounds. Not because there are no more women for these kinds of roles. There still are. And it is probably not due to a change in the organizers' convictions.

Why, then?

It is the fear of being chewed up and spat out for tolerating female-unfriendly practices or using women as sex objects. That happened to the London-based Presidents Club when it organized a charity event. The guests were exclusively rich and powerful men. The organizers hired one hundred and thirty hostesses who, with short-skirts and deep cleavage, served snacks and drinks.

Last year, a journalist from *The Financial Times* slipped in, disguised as a hostess. Her story appeared the next day. Men in tuxedos who let up on the brakes while drunk. Hostesses were encouraged to drink and interact more loosely. Hostesses were grabbed under their skirts and summoned to dance on tables. Hostesses were invited to continue the party in hotel rooms. Two days after the article was published, the Presidents Club, after 33 years, ceased to exist.

Sexual coercion from a position of dominance is no longer tolerated, as it was during Clarence Thomas's and Bill Clinton's time. But sometimes perception shifts and rehabilitation follows. Monica Lewinsky is now recognized as a seminal #MeToo survivor. And Anita Hill? She is on the committee set up by the most important Hollywood bosses to rid the film industry of sexual misconduct.

She Decides

Ghana is one of the most stable countries in sub-Saharan
Africa. It is well-managed, carries out a resolute gender
policy, and has unmistakable economic development. At
the same time, the country struggles with the same de-
mons as many others in the region: widespread violence
against women, child marriages, teenage pregnancies,
and genital mutilation.

In the capital Accra, the Belgian queen and I met a number of so-called 'Queen Mothers', the respected wives

of tribal chiefs who play an important role in the community, including in the field of women's rights. One of them said that child marriages in Ghana are a traditional way to strengthen ties between families. "You know that, too," she added, looking at Queen Mathilde with a smile, "the arranged marriages within royal families?"

Until a few years ago, few in Ghana had realized that child marriages were harmful. It had been the custom for centuries, out of ignorance. Now we understand that, the Queen Mothers said. Child marriages prevent girls from realizing their dreams. Nobody hopes to bring a first child into the world at the age of fourteen. That is why we want to ban all child marriages by 2030.

The discussion soon focused on the link between extreme poverty and premature pregnancies. I felt that everyone around the table was skating around the problem, and so broached the topic of family planning. Some hesitant young women pointed out how contraceptives were hard to access. Two hundred million women and girls do not have access to the contraceptives they want. We know the effect – more than 20 million unsafe abortions worldwide per year.

Family planning is essential to not only containing the population explosion but giving individual women a chance at a better life. In our terminology, we call this the sexual and reproductive rights of women. Simply put, it means every girl, every woman, must be able to decide for herself when she will have children, how many she wants, and with which partner she wants them. Because when girls decide this for themselves, they become stronger women, stronger partners and stronger mothers. It is a question I often ask women in my country: *What would your life look like if you did not have access to contraceptives? Would you be doing what you do today? Would you be where you are now?* Asking the question answers itself.

During a visit to Niger, I had a shocking conversation with a minister. Niger is very poor. More than half of the population is under the age of fifteen. Ten percent of children die before they turn five. The country has one of the highest birth rates in the world. On average, every woman gives birth to over seven children. (In Western Europe, that number is fewer than two). The population of Niger doubles every seventeen years. Yet, my colleague claimed, the future would show that having so many children was a good thing for his country. The demographic explosion will bring us luck, he assured me.

Irresponsible and grotesque. Today, there are 20 million Nigeriens. If nothing happens, then there will be 80 million in 2050. How all those people will get enough to eat and receive sufficient medical care, as well as become trained and employed, nobody knows. The country has no natural resources, no industry, no investments, no tourism. It is almost entirely dependent on foreign aid and on the money that emigrant Nigeriens send their relatives. That will be the choice for the next generations in that country: surviving in poverty or emigrating ... and all this with a politician encouraging the women of Niger to have as many children as possible.

It is more than grotesque, it is criminal. In Africa, the population will double by 2050 to more than two billion. After 2050, Africa will be the only continent where the population will continue to increase. One in four people on earth will be an African. This demographic explosion is the largest burden on the economic and human development of that continent. No economy can create enough jobs and prosperity to keep pace with such a population increase. No society can build schools and hospitals at that rate. And no donor organization can offer a solution to a population that grows so quickly. I understand that such a young population can be a great source of wealth for these countries, provided that there are sufficient economic prospects for the young, and that, as these countries grow, the population growth will decrease. In a dynamic country like Kenya, there is a demographic dividend, but not in the desert land of Niger.

The people in African countries, especially the women, understand this. These are women who want fewer children. They realize that too many children primarily means too many poor children. They know that they do not benefit from so many children; too many children at a young age puts the brakes on their own development, on their prospects for education and employment. Having too many children shackles them to the home. Too many children means dying earlier; their malnourished bodies are not designed for so many pregnancies. Every day eight hundred girls and women die of preventable complications during pregnancy and childbirth. That is the equivalent of three full planes crashing, every single day.

In many countries, becoming a mother is the most dangerous thing you can do during your life. In Afghanistan, one in eleven births or pregnancies is fatal for the mother. In Sweden, the figure is one in eleven thousand. For every fourteen girls born in Somalia or Chad, there is one that will lose her life during childbirth.

And yet, after taking office, President Trump once again introduced the Global Gag Rule. With one stroke of the pen, he forbade the American government supporting organizations that defend the right to abortion and family planning. Thanks to this decision, organizations lost more than €500 million ($567 million) in subsidies overnight. According to the NGO Marie Stopes International, this decision will have fatal consequences during Trump's four-year mandate: six million more unwanted pregnancies, two million more unsafe abortions, 20,000 more mothers who will die during childbirth.

Wholly displeased, I, together with my colleagues from the Netherlands, Denmark and Sweden, launched the She Decides movement. Six weeks after Trump's decision, we organized an international conference in Brussels, in which more than fifty countries and organizations participated. The intention was to inform the international community about the consequences of the US's decision, and to mobilize funds so that the affected organizations could continue their work. On the day of the conference, we raised €181 million ($205 million) in new funds. A year and a half later, we exceeded €500 million euros. At my own end, I released nearly €30 million ($34 million) in funds for it.

Following the conference, I paid a visit to Benin and Senegal. In Senegal, we spoke with religious leaders about family planning. I was surprised that the conversations were so open. I knew that many Senegalese men think women want contraceptives in order to cheat. We started the conversation with the argument that family planning can prevent medical complications in successive pregnancies. Our hosts were open to these arguments. If we had made a plea for abortion, the conversation would have ended immediately.

It is important to note that *She Decides* is not a pro-abortion movement, but rather believes that safe abortions must be possible for the girls and women who choose them. Decisions like those of President Trump do not lead to *fewer*, but to *more unsafe* abortions. All studies show that the countries where abortion is banned end up witnessing more pregnancy terminations than countries where abortion is legal!

In Senegal, I also visited a project that allows girls and boys to receive sex education. In a conservative country like Senegal, it is very difficult for young people to obtain information about sexuality. The project consists of a simple telephone system. Young people dial a number and hear a menu that says; "*If you want information about condoms, press one. About the pill, press two,*" and so on.

We all are familiar with that kind of help desk; in fact, sometimes we can get annoyed by its impersonal character. But for Senegalese girls and boys, that impersonal nature is a blessing. They are so afraid of talking directly to people about sexuality that an anonymous recording is much more effective. It is similar to Sophie Bot, the artificial intelligence app from Kenya that answers questions about reproductive health.

She Decides has become a broad, global movement. We have long outgrown the reactive response toward an irresponsible American decision. Instead, we have developed a positive story: not *against* Trump, but *for* girls' and women's rights, and, in particular, for their sexual and reproductive rights. When I look back on my mandate as Minister for Development Cooperation, this is perhaps the initiative of which I am most proud.

Education for Girls: My Top Priority

Since I am Belgium's Development Minister, people regularly ask, *"If you could spend your entire budget on a single domain, what would it be? Which priority would you choose?"* Most people would answer, "Make sure everyone gets enough food. End hunger in the world." Indeed, ensuring that people do not die of hunger is a foremost challenge. Others would say healthcare; make sure that people in the poorest countries no longer die from illnesses that are perfectly preventable. Tuberculosis. Diarrhea. Malaria.

Typhoid. Worm infections. Tens of millions of people die from those. Undoubtedly, that is also a top priority. But I would choose differently: education for girls. When people no longer die of starvation or die of curable diseases, this is obviously a substantial improvement. But it is not a catalyst for development. Education for girls is.

What are we talking about? Worldwide, around 260 million children are not receiving an education. In primary education, the gender gap has virtually disappeared; approximately as many girls as boys are in primary education. In secondary education, however, the gender gap still exists; twice as many girls are absent from secondary education as boys. I want to change that. Education for girls is an enormous impetus for development, not only for individuals, but also for society as a whole.

Two education experts from the World Bank, Harry Patrinos and Claudio Montenegro, study education's return on investment. They researched what impact one extra year of education has upon a person's professional income. Put another way, how much more will a child earn throughout his or her entire career if he or she stays in school one year longer?

It turns out that in all countries going to school longer leads to a higher income. The returns are higher for girls everywhere: on average 10% for boys and 12% for girls.

Concretely, this means that a girl who goes to school for a year longer can assume that her overall income from work will rise by 12%. Girls in sub-Saharan Africa who finish their secondary education, going to school for four years longer than is typical, see their income from work increase by approximately half.

Of course, more education will benefit the girls themselves in the first place. Their professional income will rise with every extra school year completed. The future families that this group of girls will start will notice the difference immediately. In sub-Saharan Africa, mothers allocate 90% of their income to their families: they invest in a better home, in better education for their children, in better healthcare, healthier food, better clothing. African fathers only put half of their income into their families. What they do with the other half? I will leave that to you to determine.

The local community, the whole society and the economy benefit from women's investments in their families and in education. Often, I have seen it myself. For example, in a drinking water distribution project in Kimbanseke, a suburb of Kinshasa. The Belgian development agency took care of the investment in the wells. But the mothers are the ones who run the wells, ensure that everything is financially in order, maintain the infrastructure, and reinvest profits in a school, library, and internet café.

It is precisely because of this great social impact that I support organizations such as UNICEF and the Global Partnership for Education, which make education for girls a central policy point.

During a conversation I had with Carlos Brito, the CEO of AB Inbev, he said that in Latin America he prefers to work with women as independent salespeople. At Coca-Cola I heard the same story for Africa. Women are better salespeople, and commit less fraud. Every microcredit banker knows that women pay back more diligently. According to the World Bank, a long-term investment in education for girls generates additional annual economic growth of 1.5%. The economic impact of education for girls is obvious. But education for girls also has a social impact, and that is equally impressive. Educating girls is the best remedy against child marriage. Forty-one thousand child marriages take place every day – that's 15 million girls every year! In sub-Saharan Africa and South Asia, one in three girls marries before the age of eighteen. Usually the girl does not do this out of free will or love, but is married off. Her schooling usually ends immediately, and her first pregnancy follows shortly thereafter. In sub-Saharan Africa and South Asia, one in five girls has her first child before she is eighteen. By comparison, in the Flanders part of Belgium, there are only nine teenage mothers per hundred thousand inhabitants; in the Netherlands that number is five. In the UK the conception rate was 18.9 conceptions per thousand women aged 15 to 17 years in 2016. In 2015, the US had a birth rate of 22.3 per 1000 women in this age group.

Educating girls is the best prevention against a population explosion. In Mali, women with a secondary education have three children on average; women who do not go to school have an average of seven. A girl who marries at the age of thirteen puts 25% more children into the world than a girl who marries at the age of eighteen. Education for girls is the best guarantee for good health and a longer life for their children. In comparison with a child of an illiterate mother, a child in sub-Saharan Africa with a mother who can read is 50% more likely to reach the age of five. Child mortality is lower by half among mothers who receive a secondary education than among mothers who have no education at all.

Education improves the lives of women and their children. It makes women more assertive and independent. For some, that is threatening. Malala Yousafzai received a bullet to her brain from the Taliban because she stood up for girls' right to education. The Pakistani teenager later received the Nobel Peace Prize, the youngest laureate ever. She is now studying at Lady Margaret Hall, one of the first colleges within the University of Oxford to open its doors to female students.

During my meeting with the Queen Mothers in Accra, which I mentioned earlier, a girl spoke up who had become pregnant at the age of 16 from her first sexual encounter. A boy, barely one year older, had persuaded her to have sex in exchange for money. The girl started her story in English, but it became too emotional and she switched to her own language. I could not understand what she was saying, but I watched tears roll down her cheeks and heard her voice breaking: this was a child whose life had been destroyed. After giving birth, she had moved in with the parents of her child's father, in accordance with tradition. She did not even know them, but she was expected to take care of the parents and grandparents of the boy who had made her pregnant, as well as her baby. Thanks to a Queen Mother, there was a negotiation between her family and that of the boy. Eventually she could return with her baby to her parents, who probably had to pay a lot for it.

When the interpreter had translated her story, the room remained silent while the message sank in. Child marriages and teenage pregnancies are the result of ignorance and poverty. Parents have not, or hardly ever, attended school, and impose age-old customs on their children without considering how devastating they are to the child's future. They use the same customs they themselves were victims of years ago. Ignorance keeps those traditional practices alive, and these customs follow the trail of poverty.

Teenage pregnancies are most common in the poorer north of Ghana, and least near the capital in the south. And it is not the wealthy, but the poor parents who marry off their daughters when they are still a child, in order to have one less mouth to feed. Or push their daughters into prostitution to boost the family income. In the poorest population group in Ghana, one in four girls has their first child before she turns eighteen. This number is one in twenty in the richest population segment.

In terms of welfare, boys and girls are usually equal, but not in poverty. Ignorance, poverty and gender inequality are mutually reinforcing. The 260 million children who never set foot in a classroom are primarily poor children. You can rest assured that the wealthy Kenyans, Congolese and Indians send their sons and their daughters to school.

The Canadian Prime Minister, Justin Trudeau, correctly tweeted: "Poverty is sexist." Poverty affects women first and foremost. That is why twice as many girls as boys do not have access to secondary education. Poor families who cannot afford all of their children to go to school more often choose to send the boys because it is considered a better investment. It explains why 500 million women worldwide cannot read or write; women account for two-thirds of the world's illiterates.

I can go on and on, but I think the message is clear: better-educated women are healthier, live longer, have a higher income, contribute more to economic development, have their first child at a later age, and give birth to fewer children. In turn, their children are better fed and healthier, better educated, and also end up having fewer children.

More Girls in STEM

The challenge in developing countries is to get all girls into school. In Europe, this was achieved a long time ago – but the work is not done. It is not the issue of whether they go to school that poses the challenge, but *what* they study.

In most Western industrialized countries, there is no longer a difference in access to primary and secondary education between girls and boys. In higher education, you can even speak of a reverse gender gap. More than half of the students at universities and colleges are women, and women earn no less than 60% of degrees.

The democratization of higher education is a good example of the social mobility witnessed in the second half of the 20th century. Feminization was also involved in social mobility. Between 1970 and 2010, the number of female students increased sevenfold, compared with a fourfold increase in the number of males. The increased number of females in higher education accounted for half of the economic growth in the OECD countries over the past fifty years.

This feminization of the student population has far-reaching social consequences. For the first time in history, women are better-educated than men. In addition, they think before they start something, they succeed in doing different things at the same time better, and they enjoy a longer attention span. These are important skills in the knowledge economy of the 21st century, which is exactly why this can become the age of women. But only if girls make different decisions as to what they study. Boys and girls study different subjects, and the differences are strong.

In Belgium, education and caring professions account for nearly half of the diplomas that girls receive, for boys one fifth. Conversely, less than a tenth of girls graduate in the so-called STEM disciplines: Science, Technology, Engineering and Mathematics. These are the diplomas that are most needed in the knowledge economy. These are also the diplomas with the highest wages. Girls do a lot better at school than boys. Their choice of study, however, means they lose that lead. They are better equipped for the new economy, but they are less well-prepared.

That, in turn, leads women to employment in sectors where wages are lower, career prospects are less favorable and social prestige is less significant. Salary, career, and prestige are factors that boys take into account in choosing their field of study and career.

This phenomenon happens across all Western industrialized countries, In Finland and Sweden, only 25% of master's degrees in STEM studies are earned by women. In Belgium and the Netherlands, the share of girls in STEM is much lower. In China and India, on the contrary, more than 40% of STEM students are women.

The different study choices made by girls and boys have far-reaching consequences for careers and professional income for the rest of their lives. It is one of the most important explanations for the pay gap between men and women, due to the fact that wages in education and healthcare are lower than in other sectors.

If we want to achieve the zero wage gap, we have to do three things. Firstly, more women must go into sciences, technology, industry and construction – and, equally important, more men into education and care. Furthermore, wages in education and care must be increased, because these are jobs relevant to social welfare that are currently undervalued. Training our children and caring for our elderly, the handicapped and the sick are essential tasks in a society. *Shouldn't we value them accordingly?*

Finland has the best education system in the world. Being a teacher is an attractive profession with a great deal of prestige attached. All teachers – including those in primary education – have completed university education. Finnish teachers have no administrative tasks. They can fully dedicate themselves to teaching small groups of students with complete autonomy. They decide for themselves how they teach, and do not have to justify their approach. There is no inspection that checks on them. Indeed, they are only evaluated on the results that their students achieve! Those happen to be among the best results in the world.

What a difference compared to our Belgian education system, which is highly automatized, where teachers collapse under the load of planning and administration, where they do not enjoy even a bit of autonomy, have to report anything and everything, and are checked on at every turn. In Finland, people are urged to become teachers; there are ten candidates for each vacancy. In Belgium, it is the other way around.

Gender norms still remain a problem when choosing a program of study. Girls and boys first make their choice of study on the basis of their personal preference. In Europe, anyway. Yet, while doing this they are not sufficiently aware that this choice is strongly influenced by their environment and social stereotypes.

Their socio-economic background plays an important role, as well as their parents' professions, i.e. families in which it is customary to become a doctor, a plumber or a baker. In addition to the immediate environment's influence, there are stereotyped expectations about what boys and girls ought to do. Girls see from their mothers that they are expected to take on the care tasks. In their choice of study, they also take into account that pregnancy and childcare will befall them, so they choose courses that will lead to jobs with sufficient childcare flexibility. They choose education and care, but also government administration, where part-time work and tele-working are well-established. It is no wonder that these sectors are undergoing feminization at a rapid pace.

If we want companies to recruit more female engineers, and hospitals more male nurses, then these differences in study choices must disappear. Gender equality means that girls follow the same training as boys and vice versa. It is a prerequisite for achieving the zero pay gap.

Are Universities Male Bastions?

In an experiment published by the *Harvard Business Review*, a hypothesis was investigated that women are promoted less because they have smaller networks than men. Employees received sensors that recorded all their movements. It turned out that men and women behaved in the same way. They developed the same work patterns and networks, and maintained the same levels of contact with top management. But the men were promoted more quickly. Since this could have nothing to do with different networking behavior, the researchers concluded it could only be related to prejudice and discrimination. Men who support men. Men who prefer men. And men who promote men.

It starts in student clubs and sport teams, continues in various service organizations and debate groups, and ends in the meeting rooms where decisions are made. Men build men's networks and old boys' clubs. The term originates from the world of British elite schools and universities like Eton, Oxford and Cambridge. Men create a network that they maintain throughout their careers and that they always call upon, whether they end up in politics, the business world, government or diplomacy.

Men's networks are alive and well at European universities; the numbers speak for themselves. In Belgium, for example, more than half of university students are women. They earn sixty percent of all master degrees. But if they want to develop an academic career, they will experience the 'glass ceiling' firsthand. It starts with the doctorate. Less than half of doctoral titles are awarded to women. It gets worse when you want to go into scientific research as a woman. In Belgium, only a third of the researchers are women, in the Netherlands a quarter.

It is a worldwide phenomenon. Only 17 women have ever won a Nobel Prize in medicine, chemistry, or physics, compared to 520 men. These figures are very much the result of the academic world's glass ceiling.

It is also evident from the Glass Ceiling Index. Academic functions are divided into three categories. The C positions are the doctoral assistants; the B positions are the professors without tenure; the A positions are the full professors. The Glass Ceiling Index compares the proportion of women within the broader academic population (the A, B and C positions together) with the proportion of women in the top academic positions (the A positions). If the GCI is lower than 1, women are better represented in the top positions than in the general academic population. In the European Union, this is true only in Malta.

In all other member states, the GCI is above 1, meaning that women have a more difficult time reaching the top academic positions, becoming a tenured full professor. With a GCI of 1.75, it was almost twice as difficult for women at European universities in 2013 to become full professors than for men.

Universities will need to undertake a major initiative to eliminate this academic gender gap, especially at the highest level. To be fair, I must note that there is an unmistakable generational shift taking place. There are significantly more female professors under 45 years of age than above. In the youngest age group there is almost complete parity. But it is wrong to infer from this that the academic gender gap will automatically self-fix. Professors stay in their posts for a long time, sometimes into their seventies. In addition, men predominantly appoint men, this much we already know. What that can lead to is what we see with the chancellors, rectors and deans. At Oxford University, where only a quarter of the colleges are led by women, it took 800 years before a female vice chancellor came to head the university in 2016; 271 men were ahead of her.

With these figures, Oxford performs slightly better than the European average, where only one in five leading academic positions is filled by a woman. In Sweden, half of the universities are led by a woman. In my own country, the situation is distressing: only one of the eleven Belgian rectors is a woman at present. In the Netherlands, it is two out of fourteen.

I find this unacceptable. Universities must be forerunners of social progress. In accordance with the *universitas* ideal, institutions of higher learning must be places where current traditions and norms are questioned instead of confirmed. Universities should be beacons of gender equality, but instead they remain male bastions.

The Fourth Industrial Revolution

For the first time in economic history, brains and creativity are more important than muscle strength and sweat. That is what makes the Fourth Industrial Revolution so different to the previous ones. The first one started in around 1750 in England, with the development of the steam engine. Coal became the main energy source, and steam trains crossed the country. The driving force of machines replaced horsepower; industrial looms replaced traditional textile production. But masses of muscular men were still needed in the mines, at the coal furnaces and in the factories. This was the case even during the Second Industrial Revolution, which started at the end of the 19th century, with the production of steel and electricity and the emergence of the internal combustion engine. The production line made its appearance in factories, and mass production finally got underway. My home country, Belgium, was the second country in the world to industrialize. Five years after the first train connection between Manchester and Liverpool, the first train ran on the European continent between Brussels and Mechelen. The massive presence of coal and iron ore in Wallonia caused enormous industrial expansion. Iconic companies arose. At the beginning of the 19th century, the Minerva, a luxurious, tailor-made car, was built in Antwerp. The Minerva was coveted by kings and movie stars for thirty years, and was seen as Rolls-Royce's biggest competitor.-

After the Second World War, the Third Industrial Revolution followed, with computers, the information society, and the service economy. Now we are already in the Fourth Industrial Revolution: robotics, nanotechnology, biotechnology, 3D printing, data mining, artificial intelligence, self-driving cars, the Internet of Things and the knowledge economy.

Modern computer science is dominated by men, though that has not always been the case. The first computer programmer was a woman, Ada Lovelace. In 1843, she published a number of codes for a machine that performed mathematical calculations and is now considered the first computer. I was surprised when I read that this happened in 1843. I had no idea computers were that old.

The history of computers is full of female pioneers. Joan Clarke built a computer together with Alan Turing during the Second World War that broke the German Enigma code, shortening the war by many months. After the war, Admiral Grace Hopper initiated the development of COBOL, one of the first programming languages. Elsie Schutter founded the first software company where only female programmers worked.

In 1967, an article appeared in *Cosmopolitan* magazine entitled *The Computer Girls*, in which computer science was advertised as an excellent career choice for women: "Now have come the big, dazzling computers – and a whole new kind of work for women: programming. And if it doesn't sound like women's work – well, it just is."

Initially, women kept pace with men in the computer world. Men focused on the hardware, the machines, while women focused on the software, the programs. Up until the mid-1980s, more than a third of computer science degrees in the United States were awarded to women. A few years later, this number had suddenly halved. What exactly happened there, around 1985?

That is when the first home computers were put on the market. Landmark devices such as the Commodore 64, the Apple IIc and the Macintosh 128K. You could not do much with them, save doing a bit of word processing or playing a few games. The computers were put on the market as toys for boys, with games for boys, at least, according to the usual norms. Cars and guns. A fat yellow jaw that ate red balls. Parents bought these apparatuses for their sons. And so developed the image of nerds and geeks who wrote their own computer programs squirreled in their rooms while their sisters giggled and shopped for colorful dresses or hung out on the beach.

In a few years, boys accumulated a competitive advantage. When they arrived at university to study computer science, boys were well-acquainted with computers and programming, while this was all new to girls.

The consequences are still evident thirty years later. Silicon Valley is dominated by men, with a distinctly female-unfriendly culture, and populated with computing role models such as Bill Gates, Steve Jobs and Mark Zuckerberg. Women constitute a minority of technical staff. In 2015, only 20% of the engineers at Apple were women, 17% at Google, 15% at Facebook, 10% at Twitter and 6% at Uber.

Bloomberg journalist Emily Chang describes Silicon Valley as a sexist man's world, in which women are systematically paid worse and are constantly confronted with boundary-crossing behavior. She is not the only one to decry it. Think of the young software programmer at Uber, Susan Fowler, and her blog post about the widespread unwanted sexual behavior at Uber. Or the many studies that show how almost all women in the tech industry are faced with sexism, inappropriate comments, and unwanted advances.

In 2016, Microsoft thought it reasonable to hire young women at a party in San Francisco to dance on the stage in skimpy skirts and bras. And in 2017, a software engineer complained about Google aiming for greater gender diversity in recruitment and promotions; he viewed it as discrimination against the male employees.

Is it then so surprising that women leave IT companies en masse? You see it both in Europe and in the United States; it is very dramatic. The few women who opt to enter the computer sector are being chased away by the sexual misconduct and misogynous environment.

Women should benefit from the Fourth Industrial Revolution,

with their higher level of education, their natural predisposition to multitasking, and their ability to concentrate for longer. Too few study computer sciences, and they are underrepresented in IT companies. Often women with a STEM diploma do not end up in a STEM profession; whereas half of the male STEM graduates end up working in the sector, it is barely a third of females.

Women fail to start because they take into account their future family obligations in their choice of career. They stop because of the female-unfriendly corporate culture. A third of the female employees in Silicon Valley have stated that they have feared for their physical safety on at least one occasion. So it is no surprise that more than 40% of women starting a career in Silicon Valley leave the sector.

Meanwhile, a recent study by McKinsey & Company points to the ramifications of automation and artificial intelligence: one fifth of all jobs will disappear. For countries that manage this well, this does not have to be a problem. Nearly the entire loss of employment can be offset by the creation of new jobs in digital technology. But many more girls will need to study computer science to fill the vacancies here.

We will also have to be careful that gender norms do not creep into the algorithms and neural networks of artificial intelligence. It is a field where even fewer women work than in the rest of the technology sector.

Artificial intelligence is based upon available data, not rules. Masses of data are analyzed, but the results are only as accurate as the data on which they are based. It is a problem known as SISO: *Shit In, Shit Out.* The input determines the output. If the data entered are not gender-neutral, then the decisions based on those algorithms will not be either. If such an algorithm assumes that top jobs are predestined for men and housework for women, then you can imagine what that means for the decisions made by banks, investors, insurance companies, educational institutions and the government.

Silicon Valley finally seems to understand that it is shooting itself in the foot. Just ask Travis Kalanick, Uber's founder, who had to leave his own company because of the sexist corporate culture. While the tech sector promises improvement, it still has a long way to go. Two things seem imperative to me: making the extent of gender inequality public – identifying problems is the first step to fixing them – and then developing gender diversity programs based on the data. These are currently too anecdotal, and based on gut feeling.

All companies, not just those in tech, should better investigate what is happening to their female employees. They have tons of data on recruitment, salaries, sabbaticals and promotions, and the statistical information can be used to track the courses of careers and salaries. Data breeds awareness. Where is the prejudice? Where is the discrimination? Such information will help companies realize the full potential of their female employees.

Last year, the World Economic Forum in Davos focused specifically on gender equality. WEF Executive Chairman Klaus Schwab appointed as many as seven female co-chairs. A nice gesture, but at the same time an indication that the WEF also has a problem in that area: only 21% of the participants were women; a record, but still very low.

I heard a speech by Robert Smith, from Vista Equity Partners, a fund that invests in technology companies. Within each company that Vista Equity Partners invests in, they have determined that the female talent is underutilized. Smith launched a program, *Liberate the Talent*, which tests the skills of all lower- and middle-management employees in these companies. Time and time again, women were discovered who have the talent to grow into top jobs but nevertheless remained under the radar. Smith calls them *hidden gems*.

The Vista Equity Partners investment fund has three hundred investors. None of them ever asks a question about diversity and gender equality, Smith said. He made the comparison with ethical investing. This has been so successful that every company now has an ESG policy (environmental, social and governance criteria) for investments. If investors were to attach the same importance to diversity and gender equality, then all companies would also develop a policy for this. "Money drives policy" Smith concluded. This must also be the case for gender equality.

Scandinavia as a Role Model?

On October 24, 1975, women went on strike in Iceland. They refused to work, cook, clean or take care of children. As many as 90% of all Icelandic women took part. That day they did not lift a finger, and held a massive demonstration in Reykjavik. The entire nation came to a standstill. Factories, schools, hospitals, shops and government institutions had to close their doors. Men suddenly had to make breakfast, change diapers, take care of children (because they could not go to school), and do the shopping. All of which meant they could not get to work themselves.

In one day, it became clear that women might not have too much to say in economics or in politics, but that life completely ground to a halt when they stopped doing what they did every day – and what men were oblivious to. That was the whole point of the strike: showing how their contribution to society went unappreciated.

It was a tectonic shift. People speak of the era before that October 24th more than forty years ago and the era after. Five years after the strike, Vigdís Finnbogadóttir became the first woman in the world to become a democratically-elected president. She would stay in office for 16 years. Twice she was reappointed without election because of the lack of an opposing candidate. In 1983, the feminist party won three seats in parliament.

Iceland currently has its second female prime minister. In the WEF's *Global Gender Gap Report*, Iceland has been in first place for nine consecutive years, with the smallest gap between men and women.

In the *Global Gender Gap Report*, the WEF examines gender inequality in four areas: education, public health, and economic and political emancipation, and makes a ranking from the aggregated findings. The list is dominated by the Scandinavian countries, with Iceland, Norway,

Finland and Sweden in the top five. France, Germany, the United Kingdom and Canada are just outside the top ten. The United States is far down the list, in 49th place.

The report shows that gender inequality is less prevalent in the Scandinavian countries. For example, the gender gap in employment in Iceland, Finland and Sweden is less than 4%. These countries manage to attract and retain nearly as many working women as men. Besides that, they have the highest employment rates for women and for men. More importantly, men and women in these countries are also the happiest in the whole world. Numerous welfare indices provide evidence: robust economic growth, high employment and no gender pay gap are all ways to increase wellbeing for men and women alike. The Scandinavian countries are better at it than anyone else, which is why I look to these countries as role models.

Scandinavian countries have the best policies and programs in the world in terms of parental leave and childcare. Yet these countries have not solved it completely. Careers in Scandinavian countries slow down with motherhood. In Iceland, only 18% of top managers are women, in Sweden 13%, in Norway 10%. Very disheartening. Despite progressive policies, even in the most gender-equal countries, women remain disadvantaged. Even the best students in the class still have to put in some effort.

According to the WEF, no country will achieve gender equality by 2030, even though all countries committed to meeting this goal when they adopted the 2030 Agenda for Sustainable Development in 2015 (together with seventeen sustainable development goals). According to the WEF, however, it will take another century – *one hundred years* – before that will happen. In Western Europe, which is the furthest region along the road, it will take 61 years.

Motherhood; a Curse?

The main cause behind the gender pay gap is and remains the traditional division of labor within a family. Women around the world devote much more time to unpaid work than men. In Pakistan, it is six times as much. And twice as much in Western Europe, where, every day, women devote an average of four-and-a-half hours to unpaid work, compared with men's average of two-and-a-quarter. Unpaid work is mainly comprised of household work and care for children, the sick, and the elderly.

Thirty men and twenty-five women work in my office. Every time a child is ill and has to go to the doctor or to the hospital, it is a woman who tells me that she has to stay home. I rarely get such a message from a man. What are these women waiting for when it comes to telling their partner during the next cold or flu that it is their turn to stay home? Or do their husbands fear for their reputations or careers if they shoulder some of the burden? *Perhaps, their fear is warranted?*

Women bear children. Not all employers like that. I have met, more often than I like, business leaders who coldly proclaim to prefer recruiting young men over young women because, sooner or later, the young women will not be available for six months.

There are three moments in a woman's life where she has to make choices that have a major impact on her career. The first comes around at the age of 18 when she must choose an academic focus. All too often, she chooses a study that leads her to a job that is less well-paid. At around the age of 30, she will become a mother for the first time (in our region, anyway). At that moment, many women opt to take a career break or work part-time. Or they stay at home for a few years, especially if they are also charged with caring for sick or elderly relatives. At around 40, are also put under pressure to care for both young children and elderly parents. Later they become grandmothers, and are then called upon to help take care of the grandchildren. This is often the time when women end their careers.

If women decide to stay at home and take care of children, sick or elderly people, whatever the reason, they have every right to do so. Who am I to comment on or deny them that right? Such unpaid work is of great social importance. Making sure that children grow up well, caring for the sick or elderly, all that is very valuable, but it must be the woman's choice, and it must be organic. It is wrong when women are forced into choices they would make differently because of the absence of childcare, or because childcare takes up too large a chunk of a salary, or because their employer does not allow part-time work or working from home for a few days, or refuses to adjust the work hours to school hours.

Besides, men must have the same freedom to choose to stay at home. Gender neutrality is choice neutrality. It is too one-sided when the woman must take on the caretaking and sideline her career. It can be different. In the Scandinavian countries, women continue to work without their children growing up as street urchins or hooligans, without leaving sick or elderly people to their fate.

Women who decide to stay at home or work less pay a high price for motherhood. The economists Michelle Budig and Paula England have calculated that women have an average wage gap of 7% for each child that they have. Through parental leave, career interruptions, part-time work and occasional absenteeism, they lag behind in promotions, they rise to fewer senior management positions, and also accrue smaller pensions.

The Scandinavian countries have managed to close the unemployment trap for women. More than three-quarters of women are active in the labor market, albeit often part-time, but this is still better than most: it is better that women are able to work part-time than not work at all. In Sweden, the gap between the employment rate of men and women is less than 3%. In other countries, that gap is much greater. In the US, 75% of men are employed versus 64.9% of women; in the United Kingdom almost eight out of ten men work, compared with seven out of ten women. Across the OECD countries there is an average gap of 15%. From an economic point of view, that is lost opportunity; it is a waste of talent that is not tapped into and developed. It is a waste of the investment, training women who will subsequently perform unpaid work at home.

It is not black and white. Women's choices are between a happy family or a successful career. Millions of women prove every day that you can combine both. It is just that women have to make more of an effort than men.

The secret, a female top manager confided to me recently, often lies with the life partner being a *real* partner in combining work and family, too.

Women not willing to pay a career price for motherhood often go through life single and childless, while men combine work and family without too much struggle – easy if you leave the lion's share of housekeeping and childcare to your wife. Women succeed much less in combining careers and private lives, precisely because they perform a double shift. A survey by McKinsey & Company of male and female top managers from around the world showed that careers take precedence over family life for men and women alike. But men had reached those top positions without paying too high a price at the family level.

This was different for women. A third had no partner, more than half did not have children. The higher women climb on the company ladder, the greater the chance that they have neither a partner nor children. It turned out to be the opposite for men. The more successful a man is, the more likely he is to have a partner and children. Successful women scare men off, while successful men attract women.

Ambitious women sometimes postpone their desire to have children until later in life. They do not have a long-term partner, or they want to prove their motivation and dedication at the beginning of their careers. They assume that a partner and children will come later. Before they know it, they are in their late thirties, can no longer find a suitable partner, or, when they do find one, are unable to get pregnant.

As I have said often in this book, this *seems* like a fair choice, but it is not. From a biological standpoint, certainly not. Women are most fertile between the ages of twenty and twenty-five. Biologically that is the best time to have children; fertility decreases quickly over the age of thirty. Women who postpone their desire to have children until after their thirty-fifth birthday are more likely to experience fertility problems and rely on techniques such as in-vitro fertilization. That does not always work, and postponing the desire to have children then leads to not having children at all.

It is not always a conscious choice. Many childless women wanted to have children. The absence of children is the result of an insidious chain of small decisions: *"not right now"*; *"first let's finish this interesting project"*; *"next year, for sure…"*. For women who consciously choose not to have children, there is little social understanding. A Japanese MP once declared that childless women are a burden upon the nation.

Having children later in life is not only bad biologically speaking. Given the way career paths unfold, to have children later in life also is a bad career move. After all, the crucial phase in job development is between the ages of thirty and forty; these are the years in which employees are tested for their true potential. The decision as to who will reach the top and who will not is made at this juncture.

Women are regularly absent during that phase because, once they turn 30, women have one, two, or more children. This gives men a competitive edge, enabling them to push through to top management faster and more easily. Women can be accommodated by a more flexible personnel policy, so that they are no longer tested for their potential during the years that they become mothers.

Men are hardly aware of the problem. Privilege blinds, and having privilege is invisible to those who enjoy it. In the balance between work and family, it is the men who are privileged, not the women.

The Combination of Work and Family

Since 2011, the OECD has published its *Better Life Index*, an index that attempts to capture elements related to quality of life. The *Better Life Index* tries to go beyond the traditional welfare indices based on gross domestic product (GDP), or the sum of all goods and services produced in a particular country in one year. Women have complained for years that they are insufficiently covered by the GDP figures. The goods and services that women produce are often not counted, because women perform a lot of unpaid work or work in the informal economy. GDP only takes into account the goods and services for which monetary transactions are made. A mother who cares for the children at home and keeps the household going contributes nothing from a GDP perspective.

By the way, the GDP's failure to take into account the quality of life is a serious flaw. Chinese GDP is rising spectacularly, but at what cost in terms of pollution and public health? And sometimes the GDP just measures the wrong things. Take, as an example, the terrible fire in the Grenfell Tower apartment building in London: the GDP does not take into account the 72 deaths or the billions in damage. But the rescue operations, the hours of firefighting, and the demolition of the tower are counted as contributing towards the economy.

The OECD's *Better Life Index* is an attempt to rectify the GDP's shortcomings; it examines job security, housing conditions, government efficiency and personal happiness, among other things. A noteworthy criterion is the work and private life balance and the extent to which men and women are able to combine work, family and leisure time – one of the most important factors for personal wellbeing and happiness. The number of hours one works is crucial. Workdays that are too long have a negative impact on your health, on your family life, on your social contacts, on your hobbies.

The OECD sets the bar at 50 working hours per week. Whoever works more, works too long. What do we find? Across the OECD states, one in eight employees works more than 50 hours per week. Twice as many men as women work too long. However, fewer hours at work do not mean that women have more time for themselves, for leisure, for friends. After all, they perform much more unpaid work at home – the double shift.

From the *Better Life Index*, the Netherlands emerges as the country with the best balance between work and family. This is mainly due to the fact that almost nobody works too long, so they have a lot of time for leisure.

After the Netherlands, Denmark, France and Spain follow; Belgium is in fifth place, followed by Norway and Sweden. Canada lies in 20th, while the United Kingdom (28) and the United States (30) are among the lowest ranked.

Again, it is no coincidence that the Scandinavian countries score high on the *Better Life Index*. People go home at five o'clock in the afternoon, no matter their job, whether an executive or a receptionist. Their economies do not suffer, and their societies get better. Pensions and benefits are high, as is their employment rate. And there is a balance between career and private life. At the same time, the gender gap is less palpable. All reasons that explain why the inhabitants of those countries feel at ease, as is evident from the *Better Life Index*.

Scandinavian countries allow work to be arranged with more adaptability for a better balance between work and family: flexible working hours, working from home, the ability to temporarily work part-time, take longer parental leave or to interrupt one's career without incurring irreparable damage. As an employer, you have to ensure that this flexibility does not lead to more stress: allowing people to – temporarily – work less hard, but still expecting the same results does not end well.

Innovative flexible employment contracts that make it easier to combine work and family are usually of Scandinavian origin, such as school-bell contracts, for example, contracts which allow part-time work between school hours. Or co-parent contracts for divorced parents who alternate custody of their children; one parent works shorter hours one week and the other parent longer hours, and the next week vice versa.

Ive Marx, a Belgian professor of socio-economic sciences, shows that more flexibility is the answer to poverty. It is mainly single women and their children who live in poverty. That is why women will primarily benefit from a flexible labor market. Information technology makes it possible to schedule work with greater flexibility because technology allows for greater autonomy. Technology is what permits one to work untethered from the shop floor, the office, a desk, a time clock, fixed office hours, and/or strict store hours.

For low-skilled women, more jobs are needed in retail and e-commerce, which also require employer flexibility. Labor market flexibility is a pre-eminent social measure that benefits the weakest workers most, usually women. Because of the double shift, women are the first victims of a rigid labor market.

In many countries, including Belgium, the government has taken measures that enable a better balance between work and family: parental leave, childcare, part-time work, working from home, sliding working hours; though it is usually women who take advantage of them. Our society expects this: company cultures generally do not offer the same benefits or support for men who also seek a better work-life balance. And when couples make financial decisions, the woman typically being the lower-earning partner, it seems logical that she puts her career on hold, and before anyone knows it, she ends up in a vicious circle of lower wages and a slower career path.

In a gender-neutral society, as many men as women will need to use flexible solutions to better manage work and private life. If we want to reach the zero wage gap, this will have to happen. It will not be easy. When our first son was born, I was self-employed. I was able to adjust my work schedule, jumping in when needed to take on part of the care. At the birth of our second, I was chairman of my political party. Balancing career and home did not work at all, and my availability was virtually nil. It will be quite a challenge to make flexibility possible everywhere.

Information technology can help. It is no longer necessary to go to the main office every day to do your work. Our government, for instance, established regional offices outside the capital. You can log in with your laptop and get started. Many companies and government administrations allow their employees to work from home once or twice a week. Experience shows that people do not work less; on the contrary. The time they lose in the other days through commuting is now used to (mostly) work. Today there are companies that offer shuttle buses with a Wi-Fi service during the morning and evening rush hours. People log in and work, instead of being trapped in traffic jams. Hours spent on the bus count as full working hours.

There is a shortage on the labor market, meaning employees can increasingly choose who they work for. The time where employers selectively filtered their employees is over. Highly-educated men and women in the STEM disciplines have a choice. In their quest for a good work-life balance, they prioritize flexibility. This is one of the reasons I do not understand the decision taken by Yahoo!'s CEO. Marissa Mayer, the big boss, decided to eliminate remote work in the company. According to Mayer, many good ideas come from the hundreds of water cooler conversations and chance meetings in the cafeteria, in the corridor, at the coffee machine, in the restrooms. These stop when people work from home, she claimed.

Of course, there are jobs that cannot be done at home. And of course you have to make sure that the creativity and the company's mission and values do not fade. Quite a few companies do this by asking that all employees are present on one or two fixed days each week, like a Monday and Thursday, for example. But abolishing all flexibility, I just cannot fathom it; it is such short-term thinking. You shut the door on a lot of talent by underestimating the power of technology in making flexibility *a company asset*. It is a bizarre signal from the boss of a technology giant like Yahoo!.

Part-Time Work, a Blessing?

Every year in September, I participate in a number of meetings at the United Nations in New York. It is a good chance for me to schedule meetings outside the UN building with, for example, either Belgian companies based in New York or with digital start-ups.

Our Consul General in New York is Cathy Buggenhout, an impressive woman with enormous will and force, even though she is small in stature. She is familiar with my interest in gender equality and organized a dinner with approximately 15 female entrepreneurs who were very successful in their field. Women like Tiffany Pham, who reaches 18 million women with her online media platform Mogul every week. Or Maria Yuan, who, with IssueVoter checks how elected representatives vote on bills that have an impact on gender equality. Or Hanna Zubko, who provides financial integration services to large companies with IntellectEU.

The stories they shared were more or less the same: how they had to perform in a biased climate and even face opposition from their male colleagues. I was impressed. These were women who belonged to the absolute top of their domain, but who all had to overcome the same obstacles. Many were directly confronted with sexism. Men who refused to take them seriously. Male bankers who looked suspiciously at their business plans. It turns out to be true that female entrepreneurs have more difficulty in accessing financial lending. And further: the derogatory remarks, the "joking" slights, the automatic assumptions that the woman in the group will fetch the coffee. Even male hands that mysteriously appeared where they did not belong. It all took place. In New York City. In the twenty-first century. With very successful women.

I remember something else that night. Our Consul General told me that for years she had refused all requests from her female staff to work part-time. As far as she was concerned, men can work part-time as often as they want, but not women – unless the men do it with the same frequency.

She explained that women often get trapped in a part-time job, that they later fail to step back into full-time work again, that they give up on promotion opportunities, that they are paid less for the rest of their careers. Women have to be protected from themselves, she said. Part-time work seems to be the best of both worlds because it allows women to combine work and family, but in reality it is a trap where women remain sidelined for years, incurring further negative consequences throughout their entire career.

I had not seen it that way, but she is right. If we want to bridge the gender pay gap, we need to reduce part-time work for women and increase it for men. Ultimately, there should be no difference between the number of men and women in part-time work; only then will we reach the zero wage gap.

To fully understand the impact of part-time work on women, their careers, and the economy, we have to look no further than Belgium's neighbor, the Netherlands. The employment rate of women is quite high, above 70%. This brings the Netherlands into line with figures that you see in the Scandinavian countries. But what you see nowhere else in the world is the large number of women who work part-time. Approximately two-thirds of women in the Netherlands work part-time, compared to one-fifth of men. You see it in all countries: more women work part-time than men. We all know why. Women still take on the vast majority of childcare and household tasks and part-time work allows them to remain active upon the labor market. After the economic recession in the early 1970s, with high unemployment and especially a lot of youth unemployment, the Dutch government thought it had found the miracle solution: employers would receive a subsidy if they split a full-time job into two part-time ones.

Everyone applauded. The trade unions supported a reduction of working hours and labor redistribution. The employers hardly noticed a change, because the subsidy was quite generous. And the young mothers were thrilled, because they did not have to stop working completely.

Then the normalization of part-time work was formalized into all kinds of laws. For example, since 2000 all employees have the legal right to switch from a full-time to a part-time employment contract. The same rights are attached to part-time work as they are to full-time work, for example, regarding pension accrual. The economy also adjusted; there are many interesting, well-paid part-time jobs in the Netherlands. For women, part-time became the new normal.

Forty years later, the consequences are clear. Women in the Netherlands work on average 26 hours a week, men 38. When a woman becomes pregnant and gives birth, she reduces her working time to 24 hours a week, while her partner increases theirs to 40.

It all sounds very progressive, of course, but it certainly is not. The world record holders in part-time work, Dutch women still perform the childcare and household chores – the traditional gender roles. Women become financially dependent on their better-earning partners. Women see their career opportunities shrink, because a 26-hour working week does not get you into a management position. Women are the primary victims of part-time work.

It is not good for the economy. Billions of euros of investments in higher education are being thrown out. Dutch women are better educated than Dutch men, and they also graduate faster, after which they then limit themselves to a job for just a few days per week. It also explains why childcare in the Netherlands leaves much to be desired, why there are so few after-school programs, and why so many public facilities are only open during office hours. After all, the mother is available during working hours.

The extent of part-time work explains the large pay gap between men and women. That is precisely why the Netherlands is faring so poorly on the many gender equality barometers. It is now starting to dawn on many Dutch people that the Dutch need to wean themselves off this part-time work habit. The government in The Hague is taking the first steps in that direction. Part-time work was taxed in the past as the so-called *'aanrechtsubsidie'* (kitchen subsidy). If your wife has a small job, you can deduct a substantial amount of your available income as the higher earning partner. Well, this is being reduced, and in 2024 it will disappear completely. A first step in what will undoubtedly be a very difficult process.

For Dutch policymakers, it will be like walking on a tightrope. Many women are quite satisfied with their part-time job. And the Netherlands has found a good balance between work and family, as is evident from the OECD's *Better Life Index*. You do not want to throw the baby out with the bathwater. You will need to have a damn good explanation as to why the stream of part-timers needs to be disconnected. The population is also aging rapidly in the Netherlands, and there is a labor shortage. More women will have to work full-time if the Netherlands hopes to maintain its prosperity. But you will never achieve the zero wage gap if so many women work part-time.

Part-time work is one of the primary causes of the gender pay gap. It leads to lower wages for women, and consequently also to lower pensions, too few promotions and fewer managerial functions. If only one third of women work full-time, career opportunities for women remain limited to that third. In this way, part-time work keeps the glass ceiling in place. And it is a trap. If you stay too long in a part-time job, it is hard to get out. Of the European women who have worked part-time for six years or more, only 3% found a full-time job afterwards. Whether you should refuse to allow women to work part-time, as the Belgian Consul General in New York did, I do not know. There is still the personal freedom of choice. Women may not be forced into full-time labor. They have the right to opt for part-time work, or for unpaid housework. Men, too, by the way.

Improve Childcare

Why are these Scandinavian countries doing so well? How is it that they have such a high level of employment for women, and their citizens are able to combine work and family so easily? What can we learn from them? I have already mentioned flexible working conditions. There are two other things: well-organized childcare and the same length of parental leave for fathers as for mothers. Childcare is the most direct way to reduce the unpaid childcare work of women. A young mother's decision to return to work after childbirth and maternity leave depends to a large extent on the availability of affordable, flexible and quality childcare. To lift the employment rate of women to over 80%, the Scandinavian countries have invested heavily in childcare that is structured and subsidized by the government.

In other countries, a full-time job can barely be combined with school hours and school holidays, simply because there are no after-school options. The inadequate supply of childcare is the main reason for so many women working part-time. Take Germany, for example; German children exit the school doors in the afternoon to play sports, learn music, visit museums and study. This is all very good for their development, but it requires a parent's ability to transport them from A to B. Women who cannot afford expensive private childcare remain at home for many years as a result of the shortage of good and affordable childcare on top of the short and irregular school hours. Only a quarter of German children attend daycare before the age of two.

For decades, the responsibility for childcare in Germany lay with the family. Mothers with children and a full-time job were frowned upon. They were viewed as putting their own career above their offspring's development. To change this, the German government has recently shifted course. Every child is now legally entitled to have a place in daycare from his or her first year. The government subsidizes 80% of the costs. It is too early to see the effect of this policy change within the statistics, but the days when working mothers with young children were considered an exception seem to be numbered.

Childcare should not only be available, but also affordable. If childcare devours too much of a salary, it is not financially worthwhile for both parents to work outside the home, especially for low-income families. In Sweden and Iceland, the cost of childcare is 5% of the average monthly wage; in the Netherlands and Belgium it is a whopping third. If you also rent a home, well then, you will simply not be able to make ends meet. In contrast, Swedish parents never pay more than €100 (US $113) per month for childcare. The government takes care of the rest. If more countries would do this, then thousands of young mothers could start working again, something – according to every opinion poll – that they dearly want.

Daycare must be affordable for everyone; supply and demand must be monitored, ensuring there are as many places as there are children. If we want to achieve the zero wage gap, both the government and the private sector will have to invest heavily in childcare. Not only by building daycare facilities, but also by offering childcare to staff members. A number of government institutions and companies already do this. Eurofound, the European Foundation for the Improvement of Living and Working Conditions, reports that more than half of the women in unpaid work would look for a job if affordable and quality childcare was available, in addition to before- and after-school programs and childcare during school holidays.

Extend Paternal Leave

In the Scandinavian countries, both parents are encouraged to share parental leave and continue to work. Paternity leave, however, is given a special emphasis. In Sweden, childbirth entitles 480 days of paid parental leave to be divided between both parents. Of these, at least 90 days are reserved for the father on a use-it-or-lose-it basis. Fathers have to choose between either zero or the full 90 days of paternity leave. There is no choice in between; you use the full right or you lose it. The number of days of paternity leave that Swedish men take is rising year-on-year and now averages 135 days; almost twenty weeks – for the fathers! That is much more than the mothers receive in my country, Belgium.

Other countries also encourage fathers to take parental leave. In Norway, fathers get twelve weeks, in Canada five, both on a use-it-or-lose-it basis. This is in great contrast to the US, where there is no universal system of paid parental leave. Incidentally, it is not only governments that make such policy, companies do it, too. MasterCard grants eight weeks of paternity leave, and Google twelve. Mark Zuckerberg set a good example by taking two months of paternity leave at Facebook. The CEO of YouTube, Susan Wojcicki, argues that women and men should take parental leave for longer. She took fourteen weeks herself. Both leaders clearly understood their impact as role models.

In European countries, mothers have a lot more parental leave than men. For example, mothers in Germany are entitled to fourteen weeks of parental leave, compared to zero days for the fathers. In Belgium, it is fifteen weeks of parental leave for mothers compared to two weeks for fathers. In the Netherlands, it is sixteen weeks for the mothers and three days for the fathers.

Since the intention is to encourage both fathers and mothers to take parental leave for a sufficiently long period, the financial incentive should be the same for both. In addition, the system must be financially worthwhile. If the reimbursement is too low, many fathers will forgo leave for financial reasons. In most countries, we see that mothers and fathers keep around 80% of their pay during their parental leave, albeit with a limit that fluctuates between €80 and €100 per day.

Studies confirm that an increase in paternity leave results in a reduction of the gender pay gap. Fathers and mothers receive the same benefits during parental leave, and mothers can re-enter the labor market sooner.

Longer paternity leave leads to a more equitable division of household and care tasks within the family. Research in Iceland and Sweden has shown that fathers who have taken three months of parental leave are more involved in taking care of children and the household.

If parental leave for mothers and fathers is sufficiently long, this will lead to a lower number of women performing unpaid work, a higher level of employment for women, and a lower gender wage gap. But parental leave should not last *too* long, otherwise the parents will lose skills and experience. It will lead to a hole in their résumés, or they will miss interesting assignments and the promotions that stem from them. Research shows that six months is the limit; a longer absence has a negative effect on returning to the labor market, compensation, and career prospects.

That is why I admire the Icelandic model. Mothers and fathers are each entitled to three months of parental leave, on a use-it-or-lose-it basis. In addition, they are entitled to three months that they can divide between themselves. During parental leave, 80% of their salary is paid to them by the government. Parental leave never lasts longer than six months, and parents rejoin the labor pool thanks to the availability of affordable quality childcare. The bias against women that surfaces during recruitment (due to their potential maternity leave) also disappears, because men take parental leave, too.

Fathers are not viewed with suspicion because they take a long paternity leave. The reverse is the case – they are singled out if they do not. Ninety percent of Icelandic fathers take the full first three months. Afterwards they also appear to take on a larger share of the household and childcare. Iceland is the country with the highest gender parity and the highest employment rate for women in the world. The Icelandic model works and causes the desired effects.

Lower the Compulsory Age for School

Gender equality in terms of time expenditure is a crucial element of achieving the zero wage gap. The Scandinavian countries have succeeded in making childcare and household work more equitable and have nearly closed the gender employment gap with affordable childcare and longer paternity leave. Other countries can learn something from this.

There is one measure that no European country has taken to date, and which, in my opinion, is of great importance:

lowering the compulsory age for school. In most European countries, the compulsory age for school is six years. The Netherlands is an exception with five years.

I advocate drastically reducing the compulsory school age to three years or even two and a half. Why? Because it is good for the children *and* their mothers. It is good for the children because they develop their social skills and intellectual curiosity from an earlier age and increase their language skills. The latter is especially important for children from immigrant or disadvantaged families (for whom language deficits and social isolation are serious developmental obstacles). School must function as a social equalizer. A good social mix in every school is a must in order to avoid the development of segregation.

Mandating a lower age for school is not only good for the children, especially those from disadvantaged backgrounds and those with immigrant backgrounds. It is also good for mothers. It offers single women a way out of the employment trap, which is also a poverty trap. This is, of course, dependent on the schools providing after-school care (instead of leaving children to fend for themselves at four-thirty in the afternoon) and children having programs to attend during the school holidays. School is by far the cheapest form of childcare. Lowering the school age is an especially beneficial social measure;

if you do not lower the age, a gap between children who go to pre-school and the children who do not appears, plus there is no solution for the mothers, who become limited in their ability to return to work.

Help, the Pipeline is Leaking

We've already broached the issue of the lateral career segregation: women in education and care; men in the STEM
professions. But there is also a vertical segregation, the
infamous glass ceiling.

In the advanced industrialized countries of the OECD, *not
even a third* of the leading business positions are occupied
by women. This mainly has to do with availability. You
have to work full-time to get through to managerial or
higher roles. But there is also the phenomenon of the

so-called 'leaky pipeline'. The share of women decreases with every promotion.

McKinsey & Company has shown just how leaky this pipeline is. In the United States, the majority of master's diplomas are awarded to women, but at the time of recruitment, that share immediately drops to below half of the workforce. This inequality then increases with every promotion. In the first major promotion, to manager, the share of women falls to less than 40%. In the next important career move, the promotion to vice president, it shrinks to less than a third. In the ultimate culmination, joining the executive committee, the business apex, the share of women is only a fifth. Only one in five of the highest positions in business is occupied by a woman.

Sheryl Sandberg experienced this firsthand. When she started working, as many women as men entered their first job. "When I looked around me," she says, "I saw equality. But when I looked up, I only saw men." As she ascended, fewer and fewer women were in her group. Now that she is the number two of a mega company, Facebook, she has practically no more female colleagues. Of course, progress has been made in recent decades, she concluded, but not when it comes to the share of women in the top jobs.

Could this mean that women are simply less ambitious? McKinsey & Company also investigated that. Guess what? Women are just as ambitious as men. Both men and women realize that a career in top management requires significant availability, which is difficult to combine with family life. McKinsey & Company calls this the "any-time model": members of an executive committee must be available anytime and anywhere. Long working days, frequent weekend work, lots of traveling. That realization puts a damper on ambition, especially for women: *Can I do everything that is required*? Only a quarter of women respond positively to that question, whereas half of the men do. Two factors are involved. As women begin a family, they become less available, at least for some time, making them less likely to apply for top positions. And if they do apply, their bosses assume that they will not be sufficiently available. Talk about a vicious circle.

Men promote too few women. What we have seen in academia is also ingrained in the business world. Men should know better; or they should at least educate themselves. In recent years, one study after another has shown that companies with women in top management positions perform better. A study in Finland came to the conclusion that companies with a female CEO are, on average, 10% more profitable. The *USA Today* newspaper calculated that the share prices of companies led by women recovered twice as quickly from the financial crisis of 2008. *Forbes* magazine also concluded that the share prices of companies with female CEOs were doing considerably better. The same reasons are given each time: women analyze more rationally, take less risk, and exhibit less arrogance. Christine Lagarde, Managing Director of the International Monetary Fund, remarked that the economic crisis would have looked completely different if Lehman Brothers, the investment bank that went bankrupt in 2008, was called Lehman Sisters.

McKinsey & Company has shown a strong correlation between the presence of women in the top management of a company and company performance. Women bring different leadership qualities to a management team than men. For example, women pay more attention to the development of employees and to participatory decision making. They prefer to work in a team, and attach more importance to communication. These are important social skills that, in combination with a STEM education, are worth gold. McKinsey & Company argues for gender diversity in top management – after all, women and men complement each other. According to their research, the threshold is 30%: the positive influence on the company's performance will only become apparent with a minimum critical mass of three women in a management committee of ten people. Companies that comply with this perform better, much better. Operational results double, and share prices rise one-third faster.

For some reason, these data do not sink in. Only 5% of large American companies are managed by a woman. Six percent of the listed companies in the United States have three or more women on their executive committees. They all have three or more men on those committees. More women in top management would mean more profit and higher share prices, so undoubtedly higher bonuses for the board members. And yet, it does not happen. Try to wrap your head around that.

The situation in Europe is no better. The executive committees of the largest listed companies are comprised of about one fifth women members, just as in the United States. The number of female executives needs to increase, and fast. That should be a top concern for each and every CEO and encourage them to shape their executive team in such a way that it contains at least one-in-three female executives. It is the CEO who holds the reins; the CEO must insist that this is a priority. Greater gender diversity within a management committee should become a criterion for receiving a bonus. It is a no-brainer – and a matter of self-interest. Companies where female executives make up a third of top management achieve better results, which in turn lead to higher share prices. Every CEO and shareholder is sensitive to this.

Quota?

When the newly-elected Canadian Prime Minister, Justin Trudeau, presented his government in November 2015, a journalist asked him why he had appointed as many women as men. Trudeau spread his arms in a matter-of-fact gesture and replied, "Because it's 2015!" With that one disarming phrase, he got to the crux of the matter: it is no longer possible to argue that governments need to have more men than women.

In Belgium and France, women make up about 40% of the

parliaments. I mention these two countries because they impose statutory quotas on elections. There must be as many women on the ballot as men. To prevent men from picking up all the eligible seats and leaving the less interesting positions to women, the first two places of the electoral list may not be occupied by two people of the same sex. The intention is noble: more women in parliament.

It worked! With their 40%, Belgium and France follow the lead of gender equality champions like Sweden, Finland and Norway. These countries do not have a legally-prescribed quota. The political parties, however, committed themselves to putting as many women as men on their ballots. It has not led to perfect parity in parliament, but these countries have more than 40% female representation in parliament. In the Netherlands, Germany and the United Kingdom, which have no quotas and no agreements on the composition of electoral lists, significantly fewer women sit in parliament.

When quotas were introduced in the mid-1990s, 16% of Belgian parliamentarians were women. Twenty years later, it is more than 40%: 190 women out of the 470 elected members of parliament, spread over six parliaments. The number of female MPs has increased with each election. On a local level we see the same pattern: almost half of the provincial councils are represented by

women, and more than a third of members of local councils are women. The positive effect of the quotas is clear.
The system of quotas obliges political parties to look for
women with political talent. The impact is noticeable.
The elected assemblies are becoming increasingly more
representative. We must now ensure that this evolution
continues, until parliaments are completely balanced.

Still, even in politics, the pipeline is leaking. The presence
of women in parliament does not translate into a cor-
responding government presence. Across the different
levels of Belgian government, only one third of ministers
are women. Every week when I join the Prime Minister
with my fellow Deputy Prime Ministers, no woman has
sat at the conference table for the last four years. That
isn't right in this day and age, is it?

Globally, only a handful of governments have as many
women as men. The Canadian government, as I already
mentioned. The Emmanuel Macron government in
France. And beyond that – no surprise here – Sweden
and Norway. These countries realize that governments
must be representative, and that only balanced governments are ethically defensible. The Netherlands under
Prime Minister Mark Rutte is also evolving in this direction. His government has 24 ministers, including 10
women. Not full parity, but almost.

When I plead for full gender equality in government, I regularly receive strange replies. "Ministerial functions should go to the most competent?" Each time I cannot believe my ears. *Do you really think that there are not enough skilled women to be found?* Of course, top jobs must be reserved for the best candidates, but I do not doubt for a second that as many women as men are among the best candidates. Women are better educated than men, I keep repeating it, and now have sufficient relevant experience. To claim that "not enough qualified women are available," is either ill will or intellectual laziness, because there *are* qualified women. You just have to want to find them. There is only one explanation as to why it fails to happen: men do not want to give up their privilege. This is called discrimination.

When it was announced a few years ago in my hometown that the city councilmember in charge of public works would be a woman, quite a few men laughed. *The sidewalks are going to go in all sorts of directions*, they scoffed. The opposite was true. She did an exceptional job.

Many countries are celebrating the centenary of women's suffrage becoming law. In the United Kingdom and Germany that was the case in 2018. In Sweden it was 2019, in the Netherlands it will be in 2022.

In my country, we always make things that little bit more complicated. In 1919, female suffrage was introduced for the local councils. In 1921, complete women's suffrage was written into the Constitution – but it was also determined that women would only be able to exercise that constitutional right once parliament had approved a special law by a two-thirds majority. The wait for this to happen was 27 years long, until 1948 and – although I am not particularly proud to say this – it was primarily my party, the Liberals, who were responsible for the delay. Women had to vote for the first time during the parliamentary elections of 1949. I say *"had to"* because in Belgium voting is compulsory, not just "a right". Suddenly, it went from a ban to an obligation for Belgian women.

Now, in 2019, it has been 70 years since women could first vote in parliamentary elections. This is the perfect moment to achieve parity across the many governments that we have in Belgium. There should be as many female ministers as men. It would be the final phase of the evolution toward electoral parity which began a hundred years ago when women could vote for the first time, albeit only in local elections.

Politics must take the lead in this debate and set an example. But it will have to be imposed, I fear – even if only temporarily – because otherwise it will take too long. This has to do with the fact that politics indeed is a zero-sum game. The maximum number of ministerial functions is prescribed by law. One female minister more automatically means one male minister less. Men will not hand over their advantageous position just like that.

Governments that are fully representative and gender-equal are better governments. That is my conviction. For the second time in a row, I am part of a coalition government as a Deputy Prime Minister. I prefer the current government to the previous one, because present government policy is more in line with my ideology, convictions and political analyses. But the dynamics within the previous government were different, because there were two female Deputy Prime Ministers at the table. And they were no pushovers, either; on the contrary, they were true battle-axes. I would often be at loggerheads with them, but it was different, more respectful. Now it is too much like a men's club, with the tone, comments and jokes that typically arise when only men are sitting around the table.

Quotas are also being experimented with in the private sector. However, lawmakers have made the mistake of targeting boards instead of executive committees. In Europe, one third of the members of boards of directors of listed companies are women, but that number is only a fifth in the United States. How that came to be is easy to see. Eight European countries have introduced legally enforceable quotas for women on the boards of directors. These quotas range from 30% in Germany to 40% in Norway and France. This group of eight countries have also either achieved these objectives or are close to them.

I am not in favor of mandatory quotas in boards of directors or executive committees, because I do not think it appropriate for a government to impose how companies should be organized. Not because of the traditional arguments against quotas. There are certainly enough qualified women available. Quotas in no way lead to discrimination against better-qualified men in favor of less suitable women. If women do not succeed despite their skills, it is because men do not allow it. This is absolutely the case. Women who have managed to make it into the cold, hard man's world and think that every other woman should be able to make it on their own, too, frequently underestimate this.

Politicians do not have to impose quotas on the business world because the business case for gender diversity in top management is so clear and convincing. A New York think tank, the Center for Talent Innovation, has demonstrated through its research that gender diversity in top management is crucial to making the right business decisions and drive innovation. Actually, it is nothing more than healthy common sense. Half of consumers are women. Up to 70% of purchase decisions in a family are made or influenced by a woman, even if it concerns the family car or the laptop. It's no surprise that gender diversity in management leads to better market results. Know your customer!

The fact that a company has as many women as men in its executive committee demonstrates foresight. It is far more important for business results to have sufficient women on the executive committee than on the board of directors. Quotas for the boards are a sideshow, as *The Economist* once wrote. The real importance, from an economic point of view, is at least a third – and ideally half – of the top management on the executive committee being women.

Change is borne by people who set the stage; the business world also needs a Trudeau or a Macron, leaders who are able to succeed in making something that has been unfulfilled for years suddenly become inevitable.

Affirmative action can help. If two candidates have the same skills and expertise, and are equally suitable, recruitment or promotion should go to the woman. Companies are better off, because they perform better with greater gender diversity.

I prefer affirmative action over positive discrimination. Positive discrimination means that you systematically favor women (or men in certain situations) in terms of recruitment and promotions, whether they possess the required skills or not. Positive discrimination casts a shadow over every woman's recruitment or promotion. It makes men drop out. One evil does not justify the other; you cannot substitute discrimination against women with a new form.

Why not reach that goal through a financial stimulus? No more bonuses for executives until gender diversity goals are met. When men feel it in their wallets, they will quickly take action. That is exactly what happened at PepsiCo in 2002, when the bonuses of the executives were not paid in full. The goal of achieving 50 percent diversity in recruitment had not been met. Since then, this target has been achieved, year after year, and the bonuses have been paid out in full, year after year, too.

Quota?

Women or Immigrants?

There is an indisputable business case for gender diversity, not only from a company perspective but also from a macroeconomic perspective. Female talent is the most important underused natural resource we have. Worldwide, only 45% of women are in formal employment. That means 715 million fewer women are in a paid job than men. This explains why women contribute only 37% to the gross global product. Too few women have a paid job, too few women work full-time, and too few women work at the level of their skillset. What a waste of talent and waste of investment; well-educated women do not advance enough on the career path toward the well-paid sectors and executive positions.

Now one can ask: *What does it matter? Our economy is running at full speed. Unemployment is historically low.* Well, it matters a lot in the light of the aging population that is happening at full speed in Europe. All European countries have a reverse age pyramid. The share of older people is increasing, to the detriment of young people. More people over 60 live in Belgium than young people under the age of twenty – a quarter of a million more.

The average number of children per woman is significantly lower in all European countries than the replacement ratio of 2.1. In order to maintain a population with a healthy balance between young people and the elderly, every woman has to give birth to an average of 2.1 children. In most European countries, the actual birth rate fluctuates between 1.7 and 1.9. In Germany, it has fallen below 1.5. That is putting a heavy burden on the financial and economic health of our countries. The population is aging in front of our eyes, with fewer people working and able to finance the social security and pensions of more and more non-workers. A growing number of companies are not filling their vacancies. We all notice it: for example, in the hospital in my neighborhood, three foreign ER doctors have been employed.

That is an acute problem. In 2040, the European Union expects a deficit of 24 million workers. It gives us only three options. We can accept the aging population and the associated effects of economic growth stalling and prosperity decreasing, in turn accepting that our children will be less prosperous than ourselves. This seems fanciful. Or we open our borders to allow the immigration of tens of millions of skilled workers. A system of green cards, such those used by the United States, Canada and Australia. I am convinced that Europe will not be able to avoid such a system. It is better to set up a well-thought-out immigration system to replace the immigration jungle of today, where the law of the strongest, the most violent and the most corrupt prevails. But even if we do this, we will never be able to fully fill the shortage of 24 million employees with immigrants. Societal resistance to this is simply too great, so our democratic systems would not survive.

So we arrive at the third and best option. If we succeed in raising the employment rate of women to that of men, the labor shortage within the European Union in 2040 can be limited to three million. Elected officials have to create the conditions to make this possible. Make the labor market more flexible using technological innovation. Offer affordable childcare for all children. Enact shared parental leave. Lower the compulsory age for primary school. That will enable Europe to address the three million shortfall through legal migration. We can *do* that.

In several European countries, such as mine, or France, or the Netherlands, there is a heated public debate on whether Muslim women and girls should be prohibited from wearing a headscarf in schools, hospitals and the civil service. When you look at it from the perspective of the necessary activation of women in the European labor market, the debate about the headscarf takes on a completely different dimension. I am not naive; there are undoubtedly many women who wear the headscarf against their will, but does a headscarf ban bring these women relief?

A good friend and colleague of mine, Bart Somers, the Mayor of Mechelen, Belgium, who won the World Mayor Prize in 2016, summarized it perfectly when he stated that he would rather see Muslim women with a headscarf behind the administrative counters in his town hall than no Muslim women at all. Better a woman with a headscarf who works than a woman without a headscarf at home. This is what the debate should be about. Of the 40% of women in Belgium who do not have a paid job, a significant proportion are of an immigrant background. We also need to activate them. We need every talent – even when that talent wears a headscarf. Are immigrant women stimulated to work outside their home when we forbid them from wearing their headscarves at their workplace? I do not believe so. Women who wear headscarves out of conviction will stay home out of conviction. Women who are forced to wear a headscarf will not suddenly receive permission to take them off because of their job. Working women who wear a headscarf are given more opportunities to develop, to become more assertive and independent. And who knows? Perhaps maybe one day strong enough to take off their headscarves, if they want to.

In Canada, Scandinavia and almost all European countries, there is no headscarf ban whatsoever. In the Netherlands, the ban applies only to judges and civil servants in uniform, such as agents and military personnel. In the United States, the freedom to wear a headscarf is protected by the First Amendment of the Constitution. On my many journeys, I have met many impressive women who wear a headscarf for religious or cultural reasons. Take Amina Mohamed, the number two at the United Nations and the inspiration behind the 2030 Agenda for Sustainable Development. She is a fierce champion of women's rights, but you will never catch her without a headscarf. Who am I to ask if she wears the headscarf out of conviction or obligation? Just the idea that Amina would wear something because she *has* to is unimaginable to me!

The Zero Wage Gap

Incentivizing women, increasing their employment rate, this is the recipe for removing the gender pay gap. There are seven reasons why women earn less. They opt for courses of study leading to underpaid professions. As a result, they end up in underpaid professional sectors. They account for the lion's share of unpaid work. They comprise too great a proportion of the part-time workforce. They move upwards into top positions at insufficient rates. They do not negotiate their salaries vigorously enough.

Plus, there are cases of outright discrimination, where they are paid less for the same work.

We see the latter clearly illustrated in the removal of Kevin Spacey from a movie due to sexual misconduct. The two protagonists, Mark Wahlberg and Michelle Williams, had to reshoot a number of key scenes. It was 10 days of work. Williams earned less than $1000 while Wahlberg received $1.5 million.

Similarly, the British broadcaster BBC announced its best-paid presenters in the summer of 2017. The first seven were men, the eighth a woman. Even though she worked equally hard and did the same job, she earned around five times less than her best-paid male colleague. The uproar of female staff was enormous. In an open letter they demanded the pay gap to be closed before the end of the year. This did not happen, and one result of this was that Carrie Gracie, Editor-in-Chief for China, re-signed. Her male colleagues earned 50% more than she did! These were not issues revolving around part-time work or diminished availability due to childcare respon-sibilities. This is pure discrimination in which women did the same job, with the same amount of dedication and talent, but were paid 50% to 80% less.

A political response could not be postponed. Since April 2018, all UK companies, government agencies and non-profit organizations with more than 250 employees must publish figures on their gender pay gap. These figures confirm what we already knew. In only 3% of the companies was the pay gap non-existent between men and women. In 14%, the pay gap was in favor of women. In all other cases, it was in favor of men. This pay gap averages 16%, the outlier being the textile group Rectella with a whopping 88 %. There was not one sector where women were paid better than men.

By now we know the causes. More men in higher positions, more women in part-time work. The example of the low cost carrier EasyJet is striking. The gender pay gap amounts to 45%. The pilots have the highest wages, on average £92,000 per year. Six percent of those pilots are women. The cabin crew earns an average of £25,000 annually. Seventy percent of the cabin crew are women.

When these figures were published, it caused a shockwave. Everyone suspected that it was bad, but *that* bad? Many companies promised that they would act. The government announced that it would monitor progress carefully. If there were to be no noticeable improvement the next year, obligations and penalties would follow.

More countries should legally mandate this transparency in the annual reports of companies, administrations, universities, non-profit organizations and similar. After all, transparency is a necessary step in achieving the zero wage gap.

The zero wage gap presupposes five things: 1) An equal number of men and women are in unpaid, part-time and full-time work. 2) As many women as men are in leadership positions. 3) As many women as men are employed in the STEM jobs of the future. 4) As many men as women are in education and care. 5) A better balance between career and private life for women and for men alike exists.

It will mean a true cultural change, but the Scandinavian countries prove that it is possible. We do not have a choice, by the way. After all, there is a clear correlation between economic performance, social development, and gender equality. Competitive countries and companies spearhead gender equality throughout their policies and activate all talent. Those who fail to do so will fall behind, especially now that women have more advantages in this century than men, and more assets than *ever* before.

Many countries and companies are embarking on the Age of Women. It is important to be part of it. In the coming years, the zero wage gap will be a central focus. In Iceland, from 2018 onwards, it will be illegal to pay men more than women for the same work. All companies and government bodies with more than 25 employees must obtain a certificate on equal pay for equal work; they have been given four years' time to adjust. By 2022, the Icelandic government wants to achieve the zero wage gap. It would be the first country to succeed, leading the way once again. The cream is in the coffee, so to speak, and other countries will soon have to follow. President Macron has also announced that he wants to eliminate the pay gap by 2022.

The Icelandic certificate is certainly a step forward, but it is not enough. The objective must be more ambitious. No more pay differences, indeed. But also no leaking pipelines, no glass ceilings. An end to "career highways for women with so many off ramps and so few on-ramps," as the American labor specialist Nancy Rankin articulates so well.

For PricewaterhouseCoopers, the gender pay gap is also the best central measurement instrument for economic gender equality. PwC praises Belgium for our small pay gap. Almost nobody does better. According to PwC, Belgium can completely close this pay gap in 20 years, and be one of the very first countries to do so. The Netherlands needs another fifty years, Germany, three hundred.

PwC's analysis is encouraging, but we must be more daring. In 2015, we agreed with 193 countries within the United Nations to achieve gender equality by 2030. It is the Fifth Objective on the 2030 Agenda for Sustainable Development. We have promised to achieve it, and we know we can.

So let's just do it.

Epilogue

I don't watch television much. During my childhood there was no television set in the house; my parents both felt that you could do more interesting things than stare at the 'idiot box'. Sometimes it was annoying when I couldn't talk about a football game or new series on the playground. But I got a lot in return. I owe my fascination with progress and technology to reading a lot about it or working with it as a child. I have learned to listen to people because my childhood home's front door was always open; different people stopped by and there was plenty of conversation.

My wife and I try to pass that on to our sons: the world is so much wider than the biggest television screen. Our youngest is six. He knows the whole globe by heart, and can name every country and its capital city. When I come home from a trip abroad, he asks which countries I have visited, and proudly rattles off the capitals.

Now, let me be honest, we more-or-less succeed in keeping our sons away from the television, but not from the tablet. They have that in common with their father.

I still do not watch a lot of television. But occasionally I sometimes catch a series. One of my favorites is *Mad Men*, a show about advertising executives in New York that brilliantly sketches what life for women was like in the fifties and sixties: the ordinary nature of office sexism, the scathing and disparaging remarks.

The main character, Don Draper, is supreme macho at an office where men are princes: their needs and desires are central. Wives ensure dinner is on the table when they come home; secretaries magically replenish of whiskey and cigars stocks. The sacrifices the women make! Don Draper's wife finds her housewife role stifling. His secretary's self-esteem is based on her boss's appreciation of her work.

Yet, strangely, *Mad Men* is praised as the most feminist television series of all time. The episodes describe how wom-
en managed to stand up and succeed in improving their
social position. The secretary who succeeds as a creative
director. Or the woman who works her way up to partner. And Don Draper comes to the realization that he
will only be happy if the women around him are, too.
What the series is actually saying is that men are not free
as long as their wives are not, either.

That is actually the essence of this book that I want to con-
vey. But I had to first discover it for myself. For a long
time, I believed that gender equality in Europe and
the Anglo-Saxon world was a fact. I remember that I
planned to say exactly that during one of the first speech-
es I would give as Development Minister, *"Let us export our
gender equality to the other continents,"* or something like that.
No less than three of my advisors jolted me out of my
blind spot by highlighting reality.

Every once in a while there are these small eye-opening moments. The fact that men exist who don't want to extend a
hand to a woman never dawned on me, until a few years
ago, when I took part in the annual New Year's reception
for foreign ambassadors at the Royal Palace. One by one
they paraded past the King and Queen to greet them. As
Deputy Prime Minister, I stood behind the royal couple

and watched. That first time, three years ago, I saw how the Iranian ambassador completely ignored our Queen – as if she was not even there. This year, I noticed an evolution: he looked at her and even nodded her way. But give her a hand? We are still far off this.

I wanted to tell this story of my own awareness, even though I know there is a difference between my words and actions. I am not – by a long shot – the most perfect person to lead this call. In my office the women take their full maternity leave, but it is still not the norm for the men to take 10 days of paternity leave. But should we wait for the perfect spokesperson when time is of the essence?

My transformation from a passive to an active feminist has freed me from a number of prejudices and stereotypes. The French have a wonderful expression for this: I was the prisoner of a number of misconceptions, *un prisonnier d'idées reçues*. As a man you can live blissfully in the belief that gender inequality no longer exists. It's not that hard, I've done it for years. Privilege makes you blind, as I have already said. You have to open your eyes. You must want to see that gender inequality determines the lives of women and men. Gender inequality limits and entitles. Gender inequality discriminates and privileges.

How can we convince men that things must be different and that things can be done differently? By hammering home the fact that gender-equal societies are richer societies, in all senses of the word. Gender equal economies and companies perform better, according to all research. But that is not essential. What is essential is the following: Gender equal societies liberate men and women because they offer a true sense of choice. Gender equal societies are *happier* societies. This, too, is demonstrated by dozens of studies.

Mad Men gives us the sense that quite a bit has changed over the past half century. But – *and this is not the first time I say this* – it does not mean that we can now lean back and kick off our shoes, so that in another fifty years equality between men and women is a fait accompli. We have gone a long way, but we are not there yet. If we let things run their natural course, it will take centuries for men and women to become truly equal. It might not even happen at all.

The arguments for gender equality are countless. I have pointed to social progress and economic profit. And morally, it is just the right thing to do. But just because it is self-evident, does not mean it will come about automatically.

The fact that gender equality frees women needs no argument. But it can also free men. Men improve when women do not have to struggle every day against injustice and inequality. In my view, *that* is the challenge we face: convincing men that gender equality does not mean a step back for men, but a step forward for both; convincing men that their freedom is inextricably linked to that of women; to point out to men that gender equality is a precondition for the prosperity and quality of life of their children and grandchildren.

Amartya Sen, Nobel laureate in Economics, sees it as "Development as Freedom." Freedom leads to development and progress. The "freedom of opportunity" is central here: the freedom to seize opportunities, the freedom to make your own choices, to take your life into your own hands. It is as liberating an idea for men as it is for women. Such freedom of opportunity is easy to understand for women. But there is a tremendous opportunity for men as well, allowing them to break out of traditional male roles and gender stereotypes. Driving your kids to school, showing your emotions, cooking dinner for your loved ones is very rewarding indeed, for men as well.

When my country decided to send female ambassadors to Saudi Arabia and to Iran, it was world news. Such a powerful signal; a signal to these two countries, of course, but also a signal to all other countries. Gender equality is not only a challenge, it is also a mission. And it's a tough road ahead. You have to dare to forego the easy way, and instead take risks and take the lead. Belgium can do this, and other countries can, too. It must be our collective ambition to join the Scandinavian countries in the next decade in achieving gender equality. It will not be easy. But it is possible.

Want to
Learn More?

Loma Friedman et al.,
> *Accelerating for Impact: 2018 Gender Inflection Point: When Women Thrive,*
> *Businesses and Societies Thrive*, Mercer, 2018.

Alexis Krivkovich et al.,
> *Women in the Workplace 2017*, McKinsey & Company, oktober 2017.

Joanne Lipman,
> *That's What She Said: What Men Need to Know (and Women Need to Tell Them)*
> *about Working Together.* William Morrow/HarperCollins, 2018.

Sheryl Sandberg,
> *Lean In: Women, Work and the Will to Lead*, Alfred A. Knopf, 2013.

Anne-Marie Slaughter,
> '*Why Women Still Can't Have It All*', The Atlantic, 2012.

Yong Jing Teow & Shivangi Jain,
> *PwC Women in Work Index: Closing the Gender Pay Gap,*
> PricewaterhouseCoopers, February 2017.

World Economic Forum,
> *The Global Gender Gap Report 2017*, November 2017.

The World Bank,
> *World Development Report 2012: Gender Equality and Development*, 2011.

© 2019 Uitgeverij VUBPRESS

VUBPRESS is an imprint of ASP nv (Academic and Scientific Publishers nv)
Keizerslaan 34 B | 1000 Brussels | +32 (0) 2 289 26 56
info@aspeditions.be | www.aspeditions.be

Original title: De eeuw van de vrouw

Translator: Justine Harcourt de Tourville
Book design: Jirka De Preter
Cover design: Jirka De Preter
Picture author: Jan Aelbers

ISBN 978 90 5718 863 3
NUR 740
Legal deposit D/2019/11.161/016